CHILDSPLAY

CHILDSPLAY

A Collection of Scenes and Monologues for Children

Edited by
KERRY MUIR

With Photographs by
KRIS JOHNSON

LIMELIGHT EDITIONS
NEW YORK

Sixth edition, June 2003

Copyright © 1995 by Kerry Muir

Library of Congress Cataloging-in-Publication Data

Childsplay : a collection of scenes and monlogues for children /
  edited by Kerry Muir : with photographs by Kris Johnson.
       p.   cm.
  Summary: A selection from over fifty sources including published and unpublished plays, blockbuster movie hits, independent films, foreign films, teleplays, poetry, and diaries.
    ISBN 0-87910-188-1
    1. Monologues—Juvenile literature.   2. Acting—Juvenile literature.   3. Drama—20th century—Juvenile literature.
[1. Monologues. 2. Acting. 3. Drama—20th century.]   I. Muir, Kerry.   II. Johnson, Kris, ill.
PN2080.C45   1995
812' .04508—dc20   95-20205
                                                        CIP
                                                        AC

ACKNOWLEDGMENTS

First and foremost, thanks to Jacqueline Wolff, who made this book possible.

Thanks to Nancy Collins and Bill Balzac and the gang at The Lee Strasberg Theater Institute in New York City, and to Anna Strasberg.

I am also deeply grateful to the following people, who were incredibly helpful: Judy Noack at Warner Brothers, Barbara and Peter Benedek, Neil Simon, Renata Adamidov, Mark Durel at New Regency, Margarita Medina at Columbia Pictures, Beth Rosenblatt at Broadway Video, Scott Kanyuck at New Line Cinema, David Blassucci and Ken Lowe at Castle Rock, Frank Deese, Geffen Pictures, Arnie Holland at Lightyear Entertainment, Peter Watson and Premilla Hoon at Guiness-Mahon, Charles Rosner at Credit Lyonnaise Nederland, Robyn Worthington at Miramax, Allison Anders and Melanie Chapman at Cineville, Oliver Mayer at the Mark Taper Forum, Clark Gesner, Eleanore Speerte at Dramatist Play Service, Jim Marcovitz and Kay Murray at The Author's Guild, Dwight Yellen, Martin Kerr at Jean-Claude Lattes, Allan Burns, Caroline Thompson, Brad Kalos, Bridget Aschenberg, Sally Wilcox, Jillian Kogan, Craig Bolotin, Steve Briemer, Jenny Gersten at the 52nd Street Project, Nefretete Rasheed and Arthur T. Wilson of Playwriting in The Schools at the Joseph Papp Public Theater, Rhonda Akanke Nur and Estina Baker-Lester at The Department of Cultural Affairs, Vanessa Burton at The Lydia E. Hoffman Family Residence, Anne Yerger and David Schmell at JHS 22, Ms. Mullins and Ms. Smith at P.S. 36, Peter London at Morrow Books, Jean Paton at Simon & Pierre, Marie Brown, Peregrine Whittlesey, Tania Farrell, Judy Boals, Noemi Miller, Peter Zednik at The Green Thumb Theater for Youth, Tony Hamill at The Playwrights Union of Canada, Terry Dillion, Hillary Gorrell and David Lee Painter at The Idaho Theater for Youth, John B. Welsch at Baker's Plays, Larry Harberson at Samuel French, Jennifer Wason and Flora Roberts, Briley Gabriel and Kris Britt at Bantam Doubleday Dell, Florence Eichin at Penguin USA, Robert Rimmer at Penguin UK, Ann Mao and Susan Rich at Orchard Books, Jennifer K. Callan at Random House, Jeanette Sergel at The Dramatic Publishing Company, Daniel Neiden, Kris Johnson and Ead Daniels, Denise Barlow and Carl Cohen, Jeff Allen Lee, Chris Sena, Louise Yanofsky (who literally balanced the project), Maria and Chris and Roberta, my family—and Johnny.

This project would also not have been not possible without the assistance of Karl Limbach and Jane Quale Keene at the firm of Limbach and Limbach, Harry Bader, Kevin and Bill at Superior Copy, the saints of East Tenth Street, Gloria Adelson, and Nancy Davidson and Saeed Sayrafiezadeh at emDASH, and Mel Zerman, Jan Lurie and Jay at Limelight Editions.

A very heartfelt thanks to Julie Harris, for her generous support of this project.

For my students, who were the inspiration for this project.

CONTENTS

CROSS-REFERENCE

Use the lists on these pages to quickly find a scene for either a boy and a girl, two boys, two girls or a group.

SCENES FOR A BOY AND A GIRL

Peter Dee
...And Stuff...

Tina Howe
Approaching Zanzibar

Kerry Muir
Befriending Bertha

Sam Shepard
Curse of the Starving Class

Frances Goodrich and Albert Hackett
The Diary of Anne Frank

Allan Burns
A Little Romance

Laurice Elehwany
My Girl

Nilo Cruz
Night Train to Bolina
(1) Clara/Mateo

Steven Dietz
The Rememberer
(2) Joyce/Darin Longfeather

Peter Parnell
The Rise and Rise of Daniel Rocket
(2) Alice/Daniel

Thomas Cadwaleder Jones
Scars & Stripes

Susan Kim
Scientist Meets Fish

Caroline Thompson
The Secret Garden
(1) Mary and Colin
(2) Mary and Colin
(3) Mary and Colin
(4) Mary and Colin

Y York
The Snowflake Avalanche

Clark Gesner
You're a Good Man, Charlie Brown

SCENES FOR TWO OR MORE GIRLS

Y York
Afternoon of the Elves

Neil Simon
Brighton Beach Memoirs

Jeremy Pikser
The Lemon Sisters

Ruth Mae Roddy, adapted by William Balzac
Looking for Corky Johnson

Nilo Cruz
Night Train to Bolina
(2) Talita/Clara

Colin Thomas
One Thousand Cranes
(1) Sadako/Yoshiko
(2) Sadako/Yoshiko

Steven Dietz
The Rememberer
(1) Joyce, Girl One, Girl Two, Young Girl

Susan Kim
To Bee or Not to Bee

SCENES FOR TWO OR MORE BOYS

Frank Deese
Josh and S.A.M.

Peter Parnell
The Rise and Rise of Daniel Rocket
(1) Daniel/Richard

Ronald Kidd
Sammy Carducci's Guide to Women

Ann E. Eskridge
The Sanctuary
(1) Amon, Tico and Little Man
(2) Little Man and Amon

SCENES FOR GROUPS OF 3 OR MORE

Jeff Wood
Suzie and Her Sisters and the Socks that Stuck

Steven Dietz
The Rememberer
(1) Joyce, Girl One, Girl Two, Young Girl

Claude Brown
Manchild in the Promised Land

"Ronald C.," editor Steven M. Joseph
The Me Nobody Knows

Barbara Benedek
Men Don't Leave

Ronald Kidd
Sammy Carducci's Guide to Women

Dennis Foon
Skin

Y York
The Snowflake Avalanche

John L. Bader
TV Magic

Jonathan Marc Sherman
Women and Wallace

Shavontel Crystal Green
Dream

Sharlene Maldonado
Homeless Monologue

Tonya McKinley Cromer
Dear Universe, Dear World

Gabriel Herrera
I Love My Family/Who Am I

* Please note that in a classroom setting, many of the monologues can be done by either a girl or a boy.

INTRODUCTION

Childsplay is a collection of scenes and monologues for children. It was compiled over a period of time during which I taught acting, along with my partner Bill Balzac, to children ages 7 - 13 in the Young People's Program at The Lee Strasberg Theater Institute in New York City.

When I first started working with children, I used only exercises and improvisations to teach them basic acting technique. But at a certain point in our teaching together, Bill and I wanted to produce an afternoon of scenes and monologues with our students, sort of like a showcase, with a simple set, music and lighting.

We had about seventeen students to cast. Larry Harberson at Samuel French suggested I take a look at Ruth Mae Roddy's books, *Scenes for Kids*[1] and *Monologues for Kids*.[2] Our students were quite excited to have these actual scripts in hand, and to know that they would be performing them in front of family and friends. As a result, they worked very hard in a short period of time to be ready for the showcase.

Bill and I were ecstatic at the response that the performance received, not only from the audience, but from the children themselves. We agreed that the project had been excellent hands-on training for our kids. Now they had a real sense of what it was like to apply all the technique that we had been teaching them to actual, tangible scene-work.

After that experience, Bill and I had our hearts set on doing a showcase for the next semester. Having already performed Ms. Roddy's *Scenes for Kids* and *Monologues for Kids*, the question soon became: *what to do next?* And so I set out in search of more "child-friendly" material. This, however, was not so easy to do. I was unable to find an anthology for children that contained contemporary scenes and/or monologues that I felt were suitable for the needs of our students.

I began an extensive search for play scripts and film scripts. Sources included published and unpublished plays, blockbuster movie hits, independent films, foreign films, teleplays, poetry and diaries. I even began to write scripts for my students, and in turn, encouraged them to write for themselves as well.

The following collection is the result of all the aforementioned collecting, film-watching, reading and writing, and, most important of all, our actual hands-on work with the children to find out what really works. It is my wish that this book become a valuable resource for finding unusual, intriguing, and enticing scripts in which the children can play.

Kerry Muir
The Lee Strasberg Theater Institute, New York City—November 1, 1994

NOTES

Brackets [ ] around an entire line indicate where another character interrupts a monologue, or where text has been added to the original script.

Ellipses … indicate where words are missing from the original script.

Four little people 🏃🏃🏃🏃 indicate where sections of text from the original script are missing.

---

1. *Scenes for Kids* © 1991, by Ruth Mae Roddy. Contact Dramaline Publications, 10470 Riverside Drive, Suite #201, Toluca Lake, CA 91602 (818) 985-9148.

2. *Monologues for Kids,* © 1987, by Ruth Mae Roddy. Contact Dramaline Publications, 10470 Riverside Drive, Suite #201, Toluca Lake, CA 91602 (818) 985-9148.

PART ONE

SCENES

AFTERNOON OF THE ELVES
BY Y YORK

In Y York's *Afternoon of the Elves*, two girls living next door to one another become close friends despite their many differences.

Hillary Lenox, a fourth grader, is desperately trying to be a part of the "The Mighty Three," a popular clique of girls at school. When Hillary is unexpectedly befriended by Sara Kate Connolly, the school misfit, her outlook on life changes dramatically.

Sara Kate is two years older than Hillary, having been held back for a second try in the fifth grade. But age is not the only difference between the two girls. Hillary has two healthy parents who take care of her, while Sara Kate lives alone with her mother, a sickly woman who never seems to come out of her room. Whereas Hillary's home and backyard are perfectly manicured, with everything almost a little *too* neat and clean, Sara Kate's house is falling apart, and her yard contains a wild array of weeds and brambles, strewn with old appliances, car engines and old tires. Yet in the midst of all the chaos, there is a beautiful miniature "elf village" made out of sticks, string, rocks and leaves. When Sara Kate confides to Hillary that the elves are in the habit of *stealing* things for their village from time to time, Hillary suspects that it is Sara Kate who may actually be the "elf."

As the two girls become better friends, Hillary discovers that Sara Kate's home-life is strangely different from that of anyone else she has ever met. In the following scene, Sara Kate lets Hillary in on her biggest secret of all.

Just before the scene takes place, Sara Kate asks Hillary for a favor. With her mother feeling worse, Sara Kate has been unable to leave the house, and their supply of food and medicine has run out. Sara Kate asks Hillary to pick up a few items at the store for her. Happy to be of help, Hillary goes home, breaks open her bank, and buys armloads of groceries for the Connollys. When the scene opens, Hillary has just returned from the store.

2 Girls
Hillary (age 10) and Sara Kate (age 12)

…inside the Connolly house. It is cold and barren; the furniture is pushed to the center of the room near an open stove, forming a fort. Dresser drawers are on end to make tables. A knock. Sara Kate runs to the door, peeks out, and opens it for Hillary, who enters completely out of breath carrying two large shopping bags.

Sara Kate	Look at all this stuff.
Hillary	*(Out of breath)* Yeah, I got a real lot.
Sara Kate	I thought you said you only had a little money.
Hillary	I broke up my bank. Forty bucks. I had to stop and rest a lot of times.
Sara Kate	Yeah, these bags are real heavy. You should have swiped a cart.
Hillary	Oh. I didn't know.

Sara Kate	*(Pause)* You didn't tell, did you?
Hillary	No, I didn't tell!
Sara Kate	*(Emptying a bag)* You got everything! Milk and cereal. You got the kind with raisins!
Hillary	Yeah. Sorry. I couldn't find the plain white boxes, the cheap ones you said are better.
Sara Kate	Oh, no, don't apologize, this is fine, really great! Bread and bologna! You got bologna!
Hillary	Yeah. Boy, stuff costs a lot.
Sara Kate	I know. *(Beat)* I got to take some stuff to my mother.
Hillary	Okay.

(Sara Kate puts some stuff in the empty grocery bag and exits. Hillary takes the rest of the groceries out. She opens the refrigerator, finds the light doesn't go on and that it is not working.)

Hillary	Oh, man. Gross. This is gross.

(She shuts refrigerator, sees a bug, jumps. Stands in the middle of the room. Sara Kate returns.)

Sara Kate	What are you standing in the middle of the room for?
Hillary	I'm cold.
Sara Kate	Yeah, it gets cold. The furnace broke.
Hillary	What do you do when the furnace breaks?
Sara Kate	First you call the oil company. Then they send a guy who says how much it costs. Then you tell them never mind because it's so much.

Hillary	How do you keep warm?
Sara Kate	The stove. Upstairs I got three electric heaters and electric blankets.
Hillary	Electric blankets give you cancer!
Sara Kate	Yeah, but if you don't keep warm you freeze to death.
Hillary	How's your mother?
Sara Kate	She's okay. Let's have sandwiches, bologna sandwiches.
Hillary	*(Looks toward roaches)* I'm not hungry.
Sara Kate	Suit yourself. I love white bread. *(Finds mayonnaise)* And mayonnaise! You need mayonnaise on bologna sandwiches.
Hillary	Yeah, you do. I think I changed my mind.
Sara Kate	Two bologna sandwiches coming up!
Hillary	I thought all you ate was berries off trees.
Sara Kate	Why eat berries off trees when you have bologneeee!?
Hillary	*(Happy)* I don't know. I saw roaches.
Sara Kate	They don't hurt anybody. Roaches are misunderstood.
Hillary	*(Laughs)* Somebody sprays our house.
Sara Kate	We used to get that. Now we try to get along with them.
Hillary	Yuk.
Sara Kate	Roaches are very clean. I saw it on TV. Before they

took the TV back. Here's a sandwich. Yippee, bologneee.

Hillary   Don't bounce while you're eating. You'll choke.

Sara Kate   *(Bouncing)* I never choke.

Hillary   Who took the TV back?

Sara Kate   That's what happens when you don't have any money; people come and take your stuff away.

Hillary   That's crummy.

Sara Kate   Yes, it's very terrible. I try to keep things paid. But sometimes, the money's just *gone,* and I don't have enough to send to all the places it needs to go.

Hillary   Man.

Sara Kate   But it helps when I send the bill people letters. I write and say I'll send them money next month.

Hillary   *(Slowly)* You. You do everything.

Sara Kate   No. I mean. I *help*…sometimes. I *help*.

Hillary   No. You do everything. You pretend that your mother tells you what to do, like everybody else's mother. But that's not right. She doesn't tell you anything. She's too sick. You're the one taking care of her.

Sara Kate   So what! *(Pause)* I learned how; I can do it.

Hillary   Don't be mad. I was just trying to imagine it. What happens with the big stuff—I mean, the big stuff?

Sara Kate   I do it…. I do the big stuff, whatever happens—I do it. I sign it if it needs to be signed I write it if it needs to be written. I talk on the phone—when it's working. I tell people what to do, and if they don't do it, I find some other way. My mother used to get so upset. See, sometimes my father can send money and sometimes he just can't. Then we run out.

Hillary   Run out! But then what do you do?

Sara Kate   I get by. People leave stuff. There was a whole cart full of food in the supermarket parking lot one time. At school there's lost and found.

Hillary   They give you lost and found?

Sara Kate   Sure, I say it's mine, and they give it to me. I go to the movies for free; I could show you how.

Hillary   What if you get caught?

Sara Kate   Who gets caught? I bet you think I'm dumb. That's what a lot of people think, and it's too bad for them. Just when they've decided how dumb I am something of theirs just disappears out the window.

Hillary   You should tell. If people knew you were taking care of your mother by yourself, they'd do something about it.

Sara Kate   No! They'll take my mother away. Nobody knows how to take care of my mother but me. I've been doing it for a year, and nobody even knows.

Hillary   *(Quietly)* A year.

Sara Kate   People are stupid. They don't have a clue to what's going on right in their own backyards.

Hillary	*(To herself)* I know.
Sara Kate	Listen, Hillary, regular people don't like anybody who is sick. They put us where they can't see us.
Hillary	Because it makes them feel bad.
Sara Kate	Yeah.
Hillary	Like the starving people around the world.
Sara Kate	Yeah, so if you're thinking of getting help for us, don't do it.
Hillary	My parents aren't like that. My mother would—
Sara Kate	No. No, Hillary. Help is the last thing you ask for when you're somebody like me. Somebody like you can ask for help; somebody like me has to steal it.
Hillary	*(Beat)* Sara Kate? Are you an elf?

(A loud knock at the door.)

Sara Kate	Oh, no.
Mrs. Lenox	*(From off stage)* Hillary? Sara Kate? It's Mrs. Lenox. Mrs. Connolly, are you there?
Sara Kate	Get rid of her.

(Hillary peeks through the door.)

Hillary	Hi, Mom, I'm coming. Bye, bye, Sara Kate.

...AND STUFF...
BY PETER DEE

Wanda lives alone with her father. She can barely remember her mother, who left town shortly after Wanda was born. Although Wanda is "doing okay" with her father, sometimes she feels neglected, and she longs to have a relationship with her mother.

Strangely enough, years after her mother has disappeared, Wanda receives a letter from her Mom—with no return address. It is then that Wanda becomes obsessed with the need to see her mother. All she knows, though, is that her Mom lives somewhere in Texas, and Wanda has no bus ticket, no plane ticket and no exact destination—just a lot of determination. She decides to try to hitchhike there.

When her friend, Taylor, sees her on the road trying to thumb a ride, he tries to keep her from going. But Wanda is set on seeing her Mom, and, eventually, the two friends reach a compromise that they both can live with.

1 Boy and 1 Girl
Taylor and Wanda

Lights come up on Wanda, hitchhiking. Taylor enters, sees her.

Taylor	Where are you going?
Wanda	To see my mother.
Taylor	To see your mother?
Wanda	What I said, didn't I?
Taylor	Where's she at?
Wanda	Texas.
Taylor	You going all the way there?
Wanda	It's where she is.
Taylor	How do you know she's there?
Wanda	She wrote me a letter.
Taylor	No kidding.
Wanda	She says she loves me.
Taylor	How does she know that?
Wanda	What do you mean?
Taylor	You got to see a person to love 'em, when she ever see you?
Wanda	Says she got snapshots.
Taylor	Snapshots!
Wanda	You practicing to be an echo, or what?

Taylor	Where'd she get 'em?
Wanda	From when I was a baby. She was around for that, you know.
Taylor	That and not much more.
Wanda	Yeah, well I'm going to see her, Taylor.
Taylor	Hitchhiking?
Wanda	Yeah.
Taylor	Long trip. Want company?
Wanda	Do I want company?
Taylor	Yeah.
Wanda	Like who?
Taylor	Me.
Wanda	You?
Taylor	Yeah.
Wanda	No.
Taylor	Why?
Wanda	Are you crazy?
Taylor	No.
Wanda	How can I show up to meet my mother with you?
Taylor	I don't have to meet her. I can go get a hamburger while you get it over with.
Wanda	You'll go get a hamburger while I meet my mother.
Taylor	What I said, didn't I?

Wanda	I intend to stay a little longer than that.
Taylor	That's cool.
Wanda	It's not cool at all. I don't want you hanging out down there.
Taylor	You might be glad I'm around.
Wanda	Taylor, you're crazy.
Taylor	No crazier than you.
Wanda	I got someone waiting for me down there. You don't.
Taylor	If she knew you were coming you wouldn't be hitchhiking. She'd have sent you a bus ticket at least.
Wanda	Maybe she's poor.
Taylor	She probably saw some phony show on TV. Pee'd her face with stupid tears and writes you a letter about how much she loves you.
Wanda	Don't you talk about my mother like that.
Taylor	You're doing fine here. I don't know what you're running off to Texas for.
Wanda	You're interfering with me getting a ride. Leave me alone so I can hitch proper.
Taylor	Bullcrap to that. I'm not leaving you here for all the truckdrivers to eat up.
Wanda	I know Karate.
Taylor	So do they. And they're bigger.

Wanda	If you're trying to scare me, forget it. I'm going to Texas and that's that.
Taylor	Where in Texas?
Wanda	None of your business.
Taylor	She didn't even tell you what city she lives in? Just says *(does the accent)* ... *"Love from Texas."*
Wanda	Taylor, you're pissing me off!
Taylor	Good.
Wanda	There's a car coming. Get in the bushes.
Taylor	No way.
Wanda	Get in the bushes, you creep.
Taylor	I ain't a creep. *(Car stops.)* Hi. Thanks for stopping. Me and my girlfriend are looking for a ride to Texas. We're a bit shaky on which city, but we'd sure appreciate a lift in that direction and I can tell by looking at you that you're not the kind of person who'll be bothered by the fact that she picks her nose and wipes it everywhere and I release the meanest farts in the universe at least once every ten minutes. *(Car drives off.)* See, Wanda, people just don't care.
Wanda	I'm going to kill you.
Taylor	Didn't like that guy's looks.
Wanda	Will you get away from here!
Taylor	What's the matter with your father?
Wanda	Nothing.

Taylor	Does he know you're doing this? Huh?
Wanda	He'll notice I'm gone in about a month.
Taylor	Bullcrap.
Wanda	Drop by the house tonight and tell him I'm okay. Will you?
Taylor	You didn't even leave him a note?
Wanda	I wrote him about sixteen...horrible...trying to explain...what? Every word I wrote down... seemed so stupid...and like I was complaining and whining and stuff...you know?
Taylor	Sure.
Wanda	I kept tearing 'em up and starting new ones. Every one of 'em sucked worse than the one before. Besides, he'd...follow me and make me come back home before I even got out of the state.
Taylor	You really want to see her that bad?
Wanda	Yes.
Taylor	I wish my mother would move to Texas.
Wanda	I've never seen her. She's my mother, Taylor. My very own mother and when I was having this need real bad to see her she sends me this letter. That has to mean something, doesn't it?
Taylor	Probably that she's a witch.
Wanda	Yeah, well, I'm going to see her and no one's stopping me.
Taylor	Okay.

Wanda	I just got to.
Taylor	I can see that.
Wanda	So will you stop by the house tonight and tell my Dad I'm okay?
Taylor	I can't. I'll be with you.
Wanda	No.
Taylor	Yes.
Wanda	I don't want you to.
Taylor	Tough.
Wanda	Why are you doing this?
Taylor	Look, Wanda, you gotta see you mother, that's okay. That's cracker barrel, jim dandy, far out, bonkers, electrifying. But I'm going to see that you get there safe.
Wanda	I'll be okay.
Taylor	No you won't and I'm not going to spend all my time worrying about you out there alone.
Wanda	Why are you doing this to me?
Taylor	Because I like you. More than any mother that found some baby pictures and stuff.
Wanda	Taylor.
Taylor	You're going to get there safe. Or you're not going at all.
Wanda	You don't have a backpack or anything.

Taylor	I put on fresh underwear this morning. That has to mean something.
Wanda	I just want to see her.
Taylor	You're going to.
Wanda	I can't believe this road leads to the highway. There's no traffic at all.
Taylor	Road to the highway is three streets over.
Wanda	You sure?
Taylor	Do I look like a fool?
Wanda	Where does this road lead to?
Taylor	Town Dump.
Wanda	Wow. I hope that doesn't mean anything.
Taylor	Just that we got to move. Come on. I'll show you how to hitch. You doing it all wrong.
Wanda	How did you happen to find me here?
Taylor	Guess I just look for you every day, Wanda. Think that makes me some kind of nut?
Wanda	No.
Taylor	Let's go. Hey, what if she's like Joan Collins in *"Dallas?"*
Wanda	*"Dynasty."*
Taylor	Whatever.
Wanda	I won't introduce *you* to her!

(They laugh and head for Texas. Lights fade on Taylor and Wanda.)

APPROACHING ZANZIBAR
BY TINA HOWE

The play, *Approaching Zanzibar* portrays the summer vacation of the Blossom family, as they drive across country from their home in New York City all the way to Taos, New Mexico. Along the way, the family sometimes camps outdoors.

The Blossoms are making the trip especially so that they can visit the children's great-aunt Olivia ("Livvie"), who is dying of cancer. The children, Pony, a girl, aged nine, and her brother Turner, aged twelve, have never met their Aunt Livvie before.

In the following scene, Pony and Turner are asleep in their sleeping bags inside the tent. It is late at night, but their parents, thinking that the children will remain asleep, decide to slip out and take a midnight walk. Shortly after they go, Pony wakes up from a bad dream, and finds that her parents are gone!

Terrified, she wakes Turner up and the two keep each other company while they wait for their parents to return.

1 Girl and 1 Boy
Pony (age 9) and Turner (age 12)

A long silence, then SPOOKY SOUNDS start up. WINGS FLAP, a baby cries and cries, an albino bat gives birth to kittens. PONY moans in her sleep. A LION roars close by.

Pony	*(Wakes up like a shot.)* What was that? *(Silence. Then all the sounds combine into a terrifying cacophony.)*
Pony	*(In a whisper)* Mommy? *(They get louder.)* Mommy…?! *(And louder.)* It's bears! *(Dead silence.)* MOOOOOOMMYYYYYYY???!
Turner:	*(Wakes instantly)* What's happening?
Pony	It's bears! Big black bears!
(Silence)	
Turner	I don't hear anything.
(The lion roars again.)	
Turner	*(Whispering)* Dad…?
Pony	*(Whispering)* Mommy…?
Turner	…is that you?

Pony	…can I get in with you?
Turner	It's so dark in here.
Pony	*(Creeping out of her sleeping bag.)* Where are you?
Turner	*(Likewise)* Who has the flashlight?
Pony	Mommy…?
Turner	*(Running into her)* Dad…?
Pony	No, it's me, Pony.
Turner	*Pony…?*
Pony	What?
Turner	Oh no!
Pony	*Turner…?*
Turner	Where are they?

(Silence)

Turner	**Pony**
Dad…? Daddy?	Mommy?…Mooomyy???

(Silence)

Pony	*The bears got them, the bears got them!*
Turner	Will you shut up?
Pony	I want Mommy, I want Mommy!
Turner	Come on, quiet down, or they'll get us, too!

(An instant silence)

Pony	*(Jumping)* What was that?

Turner	What was what?
Pony	*That!?*
Turner	I didn't hear anything.
Pony	It sounded like snakes!
Turner	Will you stop it!
Pony	It's snakes, it's snakes!
Turner	Wait a minute, let me get my circus light. *(He turns on one those little fiber optic flashlights they sell at circuses and starts waving it, drawing liquid circles in the air.)*
Pony	Oh neat! Let me try!
Turner	Use your own.
Pony	I don't know where it is.
Turner	Look in your sleeping bag. *(He keeps waving it.)*
Pony	Hey, I found it, I found it! *(She turns it on and copies Turner.)* This is fun.
Turner	I wish we had sparklers.
Pony	Oh, sparklers would be great! *(They wave away until the tent starts to glow.)* Hey, why don't you play your guitar?
Turner	Now?
Pony	It would be neat.
Turner	Yeah?
Pony	Yeah, we'll have a sound and light show. I'll do them both and you play that really beautiful piece…

Turner	*(With enthusiasm)* Okaay! *(He hands her his light and starts taking his guitar out of its case.)*
Pony	Are you scared of seeing Livvie?
Turner	Why should I be scared?
Pony	Because she's dying of cancer.
Turner	So?
Pony	She'll look all strange. Her teeth will be black and she'll be wearing a wig.
Turner	How do you know?
Pony	I heard Mommy and Daddy talking.

(Turner starts playing Bach's suite No. 1 in G major. Pony listens for several measures, then resumes waving the lights as Turner plays.)

Pony	What if she dies in front of us? What if she turns blue and starts gasping for air…? *(She makes lurid strangling sounds.)* What if she wants to be alone with one of us? What if we're locked in the room with her and she comes after us…? What if she falls and dies right on top of us…? *(There is a sudden awful noise outside.)* IT'S HER, IT'S HER…SHE'S COMING TO GET US! *(Turner continues playing.)*
Pony	HELP…HELP…!
Turner	*(Stops playing)* Jeez, Pony!
Pony	She's coming to get us, she's coming to get us!
Turner	She lives over 2,000 miles away!
Pony	Mommy, Mommy…!
Turner	*(Rising)* I'm getting out of here, you're crazy!

Pony	Hey, where are you going?
Turner	*(Heading for the door of the tent.)* I want to see what's going on.
Pony	You can't go out there.
Turner	Who says?
Pony	The bears will get you! *(In a frantic whisper)* Turner…?!
Turner	*(Pulls back the tent flap and steps outside.)* Ohhh, look at all those stars! *(Moonlight pours through the door.)*
Pony	Turner, get back in here!
Turner	The sky's full of shooting stars. Quick, Pone, you've got to see this!
Pony	*(Whimpering)* I want Mommy, I want Mommy…
Turner	*(Returning for her)* They're amazing. Come on, give me your hand.
Pony	Where are we going?
Turner	Just follow me.

(He leads her to a clearing outside the tent. The sky is ablaze with shooting stars. He puts his arm around her shoulder.)

Turner	Well, what do you think?
Pony	Ohhhh, look!
Turner	Isn't it incredible?
Pony	Look at all those stars!
Turner	*(Pointing)* Oh, one's falling, one's falling!

Pony	There are millions of them...
Turner	Did you see that?
Pony	...billions and zillions of them!
Turner	Come on, let's get closer.
Pony	Ohh, they're so bright!

(Arms around each other, they walk out into the starlit night.)

Turner	Hold on tight now. I don't want to lose you.

BEFRIENDING BERTHA
BY KERRY MUIR

Befriending Bertha is a play about a very shy girl who is befriended by a rather unusual boy one day at school during lunch time. The following excerpt, which is the opening scene in the play, depicts their first meeting.

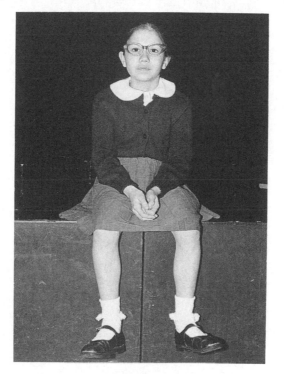

1 Girl and 1 Boy
Charlie and Bertha (both age 11)

Bertha is eating lunch alone on the playground. She is a quiet, shy girl, who is very shut down. She is actually very pretty but completely lacks any self-confidence or belief in herself.

Charlie enters suddenly from out of nowhere and sits by her. He has a wild energy, sort of like a volcano that's about to explode. Bertha is sort of shocked but doesn't do anything, just sits frozen.

Charlie   *(As if nothing was out of the ordinary and they had been talking a while.)* See that's the whole trouble with tuna fish. You eat it, your breath smells for maybe one, two, sometimes even three hours afterwards. There's a number of ways to deal with the problem. You can use Certs, Tic-Tacs…even Scope if you can find a little bottle in a convenient travel size…Potato chip? *(He offers her his bag.)*

Bertha   No thank you.

Charlie   Pickle?

(Bertha just shakes her head.)

Charlie   Sip of cola?

(Bertha sits frozen and silent.)

Charlie   I seem to have frightened you.

(Bertha shakes head "No.")

Charlie   No?

(Bertha shakes head "No" again.)

Charlie   Oh. Okay. Silent type. Good, we'll be great friends. You can listen, and I'll do all the talking. As I was saying…

(He looks at Bertha who is still quiet and frozen.)

Charlie   You know, for a girl of I would say, 11, or 12 years old you are abnormally quiet. *(Bertha looks down at the word "Abnormal" and Charlie re-phrases his sentence so as not to hurt her feelings.)* I mean, *unusually* quiet…I haven't said anything wrong, have I? I mean, nothing to offend you in any way, shape, form, or size?

(Bertha shakes head "No.")

Charlie	Or color? Or texture? Or luminosity?
Bertha	Luminosity?
Charlie	*(Amazed that she has spoken.)* Yes, luminosity. You know… *(Gives Webster's Dictionary definition.)*… Containing a certain quantity of light, illumination or iridescence…the quality of glowing… sparkling, or shimmering…radiant, shining, aflame, afire…
Bertha	No.
Charlie	*(Not understanding.)* No?
Bertha	No. You haven't offended me.
Charlie	Oh. *(He pauses.)* Really? Not at all?
Bertha	*(Not able to look at him.)* Not at all.
Charlie	Sure?
Bertha	Yes!
Charlie	Good, then, I'll continue. So…as to the subject of the tuna fish, another reason not to eat them is that some say the method of their capture has been highly illicit, immoral, shameful, even illegal perhaps, what with the growing number of dolphins getting caught in the traps and becoming extinct in the process—
Bertha	WHO ARE YOU???
Charlie	Charlie. I'm Charlie. And you're Bertha.

Bertha	You know my name?
Charlie	We've known each other for weeks.
Bertha	We *have?*
Charlie	Yes. In my mind, in the dark recesses of my mind, I've been talking to you for weeks and we've become very good friends by now.
Bertha	During recess?
Charlie	Not recess, *recesses*…dark *places* in my mind, hidden places, areas of fantasy or daydreams…
Bertha	*(Feeling nervous.)* Oh. You've got a very large vocabulary.
Charlie	I've been working very hard on it, thank you. I read the dictionary every night. Webster's (Third) Edition.
Bertha	Oh.
Charlie	I take it you're not familiar with Webster's?
Bertha	Not very.
Charlie	It's not very exciting. It has no plot.
Bertha	How come you read it then?
Charlie	I'm accumulating words.
Bertha	Oh.
Charlie	Oh yourself.
Bertha	What kind of words?
Charlie	Magical ones. Distraught ones. Ancient ones.

Poetic ones. Ones to describe the beautiful things I see, places, even people...who are beautiful, and therefore require description.

(Bertha stares at him in complete shock.)

Charlie	*(Loud voice to snap her out of it.)* Earth to Bertha, do you read me? *(He shakes her lightly.)* You're looking at me like I'm some kind of an alien.
Bertha	You're new at this school.
Charlie	Yup. Very new. So new, you could even say this was my first day.
Bertha	Who told you my name?
Charlie	I told you, you did...in one of our previous conversations.
Bertha	What previous conversations???
Charlie	Don't hurt my feelings, Bertha.
Bertha	What did we talk about?
Charlie	All about your wooden leg.
Bertha	What???
Charlie	Your wooden leg. How you spent the good portion of your childhood in Hawaii. How you're planning to join The Merchant Marines after 6th grade is over. Why you pour whiskey in your chocolate milk.
Bertha	You're crazy.
Charlie	Yup.
Bertha	I have to leave now.

Charlie	Oh, come on, Bertha…I was just kidding you.
Bertha	You were?
Charlie	Yes.
Bertha	Oh. So who told you my name?
Charlie	Honest?
Bertha	Honest.
Charlie	Truth?
Bertha	Truth!
Charlie	George Washington.
Bertha	Who?
Charlie	I'm sorry, I meant The National Guard.
Bertha	What?
Charlie	Excuse me, my mistake again…I seem to be having difficulty concentrating today…. Did I say the National Guard?
Bertha	Yes…
Charlie	Seems to be one of my off days, what I meant to say was…Tiny Simko told me your name. I asked her, and she told me your name.
Bertha	Oh.

(She looks down.)

Charlie	Something the matter?

(He looks at her for a moment. She says nothing.)

| Charlie | You're sort of a…quiet type, right? No, no, let me guess…I'll bet you're…*shy.* |

(Bertha is quiet, doesn't know what to say)

| Charlie | You okay in there? |

(Bertha nods)

| Charlie | Sure? |

(Bertha nods again)

Bertha	Yes.
Charlie	Bertha.
Bertha	What?
Charlie	What are you thinking about?
Bertha	Luminosity.
Charlie	Oh. You like that word?
Bertha	*(Shrugs)* I think so.
Charlie	It suits you.

(Bertha is silent, not sure what to make of that.)

Charlie	*(As if to reassure her.)* It's a good word…a very good word. There's others, many others you might like as well…maybe you'd like to hear some more tomorrow…at lunch again…that is, if you're not previously engaged.
Bertha	Previously engaged?
Charlie	Yes, if you're available.

Bertha	I guess.
Charlie	Okay…good. Um…Bertha…I gotta go back to class in a little bit but…um…if my Mom or Dad asks me if I made any new friends today, can I just say that I made one real nice one…and her name is Bertha? Just so they don't think I bombed out on my first day, or anything, and spent it all alone….Can you do me that one favor?
Bertha	Okay.
Charlie	Just 'cause I don't want them to worry about me or anything, you know.
Bertha	Okay.

(They sit for a few moments in silence, a little awkwardly.)

Bertha	…Why accumulating words?
Charlie	*(Picking up quickly, relieved to be off the other subject.)* Well, you know…words come in very handy, you know. Sometimes. For certain occasions. You know?
Bertha	Oh. *(Pause)* No.
Charlie	Well…for example, like…for days like today. When you want to meet somebody who…you've never met before…who you would like to meet… Words are one way that you can do that. *(He leans into her ear.)* Capiche?
Bertha	*(Thinking he's sneezed.)* Guzunteit.
Charlie	Hey, you speak a little German there, too, Bertha! That's terrific…I mean *really* terrific. I'm a quarter Italian myself, but uh, anyway…well, we can talk

more about it later sometime, Bertha, okay?...
Like maybe tomorrow at lunch, alright? Okay?

Bertha   Okay.

(Bell rings. Charlie gets up.)

Charlie   See you later, Bertha. See you 'round.

Bertha   Bye...Charlie.

(Charlie leaves.)

Bertha   See you 'round...

BRIGHTON BEACH MEMOIRS
BY NEIL SIMON

The play *Brighton Beach Memoirs* centers around the story of Eugene, a sharp-witted, quirky boy growing up in Brooklyn during the 1930s who dreams of becoming a famous writer *and* a major league baseball player.

Eugene lives with his father, his mother, his older brother Stanley, his Aunt Blanche and his two cousins, Nora and Laurie. Because it is during the Depression, jobs are scarce and money is hard to come by. Eugene's father works two jobs just to put food on the table for all of them.

The following scene from *Brighton Beach Memoirs* takes place between Eugene's two cousins, Nora and Laurie. When their father died, the two girls and their mother had to move in with Eugene's family. Nora, the oldest, takes dance lessons in Manhattan, is pretty and popular, and dreams of being in show business. Laurie, on the other hand, stays at home and reads all the time. Once diagnosed as having a heart murmur, nothing much is expected of her. She doesn't have to help around the house as much as the other kids because of her "condition." The truth is, nothing is very wrong with her and she even enjoys some of the advantages she gets from being seen as an invalid.

Minutes before the scene opens, Nora comes home delirious with joy: *a talent agent just offered her a part in a Broadway musical!* Being in the show, however, means that she will have to leave school—a fact that meets with her mother's disapproval. Sadly, Nora's mother is too weak to make such a decision on her own, so she tells Nora that Uncle Jack will be the one to determine whether or not she may take the part.

Devastated, Nora runs upstairs to be alone. Laurie follows her into the bedroom they share, and together, the two sisters try to figure out what to do.

2 Girls
Laurie (age 11) and Nora (teens)

…the two girls are upstairs in their room. Nora is crying. Laurie sits on twin bed opposite her, watching.

Laurie	So? ….What are you going to do?
Nora	I don't know. Leave me alone. Don't just sit there watching me.
Laurie	It's my room as much as yours. I don't have to leave if I don't want to.
Nora	Do you have to stare at me? Can't I have any privacy?
Laurie	I'm staring into space. I can't help it if your body interferes. *(There is a pause)* I bet you're worried.
Nora	How would you feel if your entire life depended on what your Uncle Jack decided?… Oh, God, I wish Daddy were alive.
Laurie	He would have said, "No." He was really *strict*.

Nora	Not with me. I mean he was strict but he was fair. If he said, "No," he always gave you a good reason. He always talked things out...I wish I could call him somewhere now and ask him what to do. One three minute call to heaven is all I ask.
Laurie	Ask Mom. She talks to him every night.
Nora	Who told you that?
Laurie	She did. Every night before she goes to bed. She puts his picture on her pillow and talks to him. Then she pulls the blanket half way up the picture and goes to sleep.
Nora	She does not.
Laurie	She does too. Last year when I had the big fever, I slept in bed with the both of them. In the middle of the night, my face fell on his picture and cut my nose.
Nora	She never told me that...That's weird.
Laurie	I can't remember him much anymore. I used to remember him real good but now he disappears a little bit every day.
Nora	Oh, God, he was so handsome. Always dressed so dapper, his shoes always shined. I always thought he should have been a movie star...like Gary Cooper...only very short. Mostly I remember his pockets.
Laurie	His pockets?
Nora	When I was six or seven he always brought me home a little surprise. Like a Hershey or a top. He'd

tell me to go get it in his coat pocket. So I'd run to the closet and put my hand in and it felt as big as a tent. I wanted to crawl in there and go to sleep. And there were all these terrific things in there, like Juicy Fruit gum or Spearmint Life Savers and bits of cellophane and crumbled pieces of tobacco and movie stubs and nickels and pennies and rubber bands and paper clips and his grey suede gloves that he wore in the winter time.

Laurie   With the stitched lines down the fingers. I remember.

Nora   Then I found his coat in Mom's closet and I put my hand in the pocket. And everything was gone. It was emptied and dry cleaned and it felt cold…And that's when I knew he was really dead. *(Thinks a moment)* Oh God, I wish we had our own place to live. I hate being a boarder. Listen, let's make a pact…The first one who makes enough money promises not to spend any on herself, but saves it all to get a house for you and me and Mom. That means every penny we get from now on, we save for the house…We can't buy *anything*. No lipstick or magazines or nail polish or bubble gum. *Nothing*…Is it a pact?

Laurie   *(Thinks)* …What about movies?

Nora   Movies too.

Laurie   Starting when?

Nora   Starting today. Starting right now.

Laurie   …Can we start Sunday? I wanted to see *The Thin Man*.

Nora   Who's in it?

Laurie   William Powell and Myrna Loy.

Nora   Okay, starting Sunday…I'll go with you Saturday.

They shake hands, sealing their "pact," then both lie down in their respective beds and stare up at the ceiling, contemplating their "future home."

THE CURSE OF THE STARVING CLASS
BY SAM SHEPARD

The play, *The Curse of the Starving Class,* portrays the story of a family living on a run-down farm out West. Their Dad (Weston) has gambled away most of the family's money, and is in debt up to his ears. He rarely comes home—except when he needs his laundry done.

Mom is ready to sell the farm and ditch the whole mess. A seedy lawyer named Taylor wants to help her to close the deal. But the two kids, Emma and Wesley, are attached to the land and can't imagine life without it. They hate the idea of some outsider buying their farm, just so it can be divided into lots and sold to land developers.

Just before the following scene takes place, Mom, it seems, has run off with the lawyer. Nevertheless, Emma and Wesley, continue to go about their work as usual. Emma prepares charts for her 4H project, while Wesley re-builds a door that was broken down by their father, the night before. The scene takes place in the kitchen of their ramshackle farmhouse.

1 Girl and 1 Boy
Emma (age 13) and Wesley (teens)

Loud hammering and sawing heard in darkness. Lights come up slowly on Wesley building a new door center stage. Hammers, nails, saw, and wood lying around, sawdust on floor. The fence enclosure and the lamb are gone. A big pot of artichokes is boiling away on the stove. Weston's dirty laundry is still in piles on the table. Emma sits at the stage left end of the table making a new set of charts for her demonstration with magic markers and big sheets of cardboard. She is dressed in jodhpurs, riding boots, and a western shirt. Lights up full. They each continue working at their separate tasks in silence, each of them totally concentrated. Wesley measures wood with a tape measure and then cuts it on one of the chairs with the saw. He nails pieces together. After a while they begin talking but still concentrate on their work.

Emma	Do you think she's making it with that guy?
Wesley	Who, Taylor? How should I know?
Emma	I think she is. She's after him for his money.
Wesley	He's after our money. Why should she be after his?
Emma	What money?
Wesley	Our potential money.
Emma	This place couldn't be that valuable.
Wesley	Not the way it is now, but they'll divide it up. Make lots out of it.
Emma	She's after more than that.
Wesley	More than what?
Emma	Money. She's after esteem.
Wesley	With Taylor?
Emma	Yeah. She sees him as an easy ticket. She doesn't want to be stuck out here in the boonies all her life.
Wesley	She shoulda' thought of that a long time ago.
Emma	She couldn't. Not with Pop. He wouldn't let her think. She just went along with things.
Wesley	She can't think. He can't either.
Emma	Don't be too harsh.

Wesley	How can they think when they're behind the eight ball all the time? They don't have time to think.
Emma	How come you didn't tell me when Pop came in last night?
Wesely	I don't know.
Emma	You could've told me.
Wesley	He just brought his dirty laundry and then left.
Emma	He brought food, too.
Wesley	Artichokes.
Emma	Better than nothing. *(Pause, as they work.)* They're probably half way to Mexico by now.
Wesley	Who?
Emma	She's snuggling up to him and giggling and turning the dial on the radio. He's feeling proud of himself. He's buying her hot dogs and bragging about his business.
Wesley	She'll be back.
Emma	She's telling him all about us and about how Dad's crazy and trying to kill her all the time. She's happy to be on the road. To see new places go flashing by. They cross the border and gamble on the jai alai games. They head for Baja and swim along the beaches. They build campfires and roast fish at night. In the morning they take off again. But they break down somewhere outside a little place called Los Cerritos. They have to hike five miles into town. They come to a small beat-up gas station with one pump and a dog with three legs.

There's only one mechanic in the whole town, and that's me. They don't recognize me though. They ask if I can fix their "carro," and I speak only Spanish. I've lost the knack for English by now. I understand them though and give them a lift back up the road in my rebuilt four-wheel drive International. I jump out and look inside the hood. I see that it's only the rotor inside the distributor that's broken, but I tell them that it needs an entire new generator, a new coil, points and plugs, and some slight adjustments to the carburetor. It's an overnight job, and I'll have to charge them for labor. So I set a cot up for them in the garage, and after they've fallen asleep I take out the entire engine and put in a rebuilt Volkswagen block. In the morning I charge them double for labor, see them on their way, and then resell their engine for a small mint.

Wesley   If you're not doing anything, would you check the artichokes?

Emma   I *am* doing something.

Wesley   What?

Emma   I'm re-making my charts.

Wesley   What do you spend your time on that stuff for? You should be doing more important stuff?

Emma   Like checking artichokes?

Wesley   Yeah!

Emma   You check the artichokes. I'm busy.

THE DIARY OF ANNE FRANK
BY FRANCES GOODRICH
AND ALBERT HACKETT

The play, *The Diary of Anne Frank* is based on the diary of a thirteen year old Jewish girl, Anne Frank, whose family went into hiding during World War II when the Nazis came to power in Holland. Anne's family, along with another family, the Van Daans and their son Peter, and an older man, Mr. Dussel, all lived together in a cramped attic with very little food, water, or contact with the outside world, in order to remain hidden from the Nazis.

A good student, Anne is bright, energetic, and sometimes even mischievous. When she is forced into hiding, her diary becomes her only outlet of expression. It is in these pages that she describes her hopes, her dreams and her fears—as well as the day-to-day dramas of the two families struggling to survive under terrifying circumstances.

As the play progresses, Anne and Peter become very fond of one another, and, in the following scene, Anne goes to visit him alone in his room. Anne's mother and Peter's parents disapprove of the youngsters spending time alone together, but don't stop their visits entirely.

To prepare for her visit, Anne borrows her older sister's high heels, her mother's mink stole, a pretty skirt and a pair of white gloves. As Anne walks to Peter's room, however, Anne's mother and Peter's parents make critical remarks about the way she is dressed, and this makes her very angry. When she enters Peter's room, she is still upset about it.

1 Girl and 1 Boy
Anne and Peter (both young teens)

Anne   Aren't they awful? Aren't they impossible? Treating us as if we're still in the nursery.

Peter	Don't let it bother you. It doesn't bother me.
Anne	I suppose you can't really blame them. *(She sits on foot of Peter's bed)*…they think back to what they were like at our age. They don't realize how much more advanced we are…when I think what wonderful discussions we've had!…Oh, I forgot. I was going to bring you some more pictures.
Peter	Oh, these are fine, thanks.
Anne	Don't you want some more? Miep just brought me some new ones.
Peter	Maybe later. *(He comes down and sits on the window seat facing her. He hands her a glass and pours soda into it, then takes some for himself…)*
Anne	*(Looking at one of the photographs)* I remember when I got that…I won it. I bet Jopie that I could eat five ice cream cones. We'd all been playing ping-pong…We used to have heavenly times… we'd finish up with ice cream at the Delphi, or the Oasis, where Jews were allowed…there'd always be a lot of boys…we'd laugh and joke…I'd like to go back to it for a few days or a week. But after that I know I'd be bored to death. I think more seriously about life now. I want to be a journalist…or something. I love to write. What do you want to do?
Peter	I thought I might go off someplace…work on a farm or something…some job that doesn't take much brains.
Anne	You shouldn't talk that way. You've got the most awful inferiority complex.
Peter	I know I'm not smart.

Anne	That isn't true. You're much better than I am in dozens of things...arithmetic and algebra and...Well, you're a million times better than I am in algebra. *(With sudden directness)* You like Margot,* don't you? Right from the start you liked her, liked her much better than me.
Peter	*(Uncomfortably)* Oh, I don't know.
Anne	It's all right. Everyone feels that way. Margot's so good. She's sweet and bright and beautiful and I'm not.
Peter	I wouldn't say that.
Anne	Oh, no I'm not. I know that. I know quite well that I'm not a beauty. I never have been and never shall be.
Peter	I don't agree at all. I think you're pretty.
Anne	That's not true!
Peter	And another thing. You've changed...from at first, I mean.
Anne	I have?
Peter	I used to think you were awful noisy.
Anne	*(Eagerly)* And what do you think now, Peter? How have I changed?
Peter	Well...er...you're...quieter.
Anne	*(Amused)* I'm glad you don't just hate me.
Peter	I never said that.

*Margot is Anne's older sister.

Anne	I bet when you get out of here you'll never think of me again.
Peter	That's crazy.
Anne	When you get back with all of your friends, you're going to say…now what did I ever see in that Mrs. Quack Quack?
Peter	I haven't got any friends.
Anne	Oh, Peter, of course you have. Everyone has friends.
Peter	Not me. I don't want any. I get along all right without them.
Anne	Does that mean you can get along without me? I think of myself as your friend.
Peter	No. If they were all like you, it'd be different. *(Peter realizes what he has said. To cover his embarrassment he hurriedly picks up the glasses and bottle, returning them to the box table. There is a second's silence and then Anne speaks, hesitantly, shyly. She cannot look at him.)*
Anne	Peter, did you ever kiss a girl?
Peter	Yes. Once.
Anne	*(She looks quickly back over her shoulder at him. Then to cover her feelings)* That picture's crooked. *(Peter straightens the picture. She is looking away again.)* Was she pretty?
Peter	Huh?
Anne	The girl you kissed.

Peter	I don't know. I was blindfolded. *(He comes back and resumes his place opposite her.)* It was at a party. One of those kissing games.
Anne	Oh. I don't suppose that really counts, does it?
Peter	It didn't with me.
Anne	I've been kissed twice. Once a man I'd never seen before kissed me on the cheek when he picked me off the ice and I was crying. And the other was Mr. Koophuis, a friend of Father's who kissed my hand. You wouldn't say those counted, would you?
Peter	I wouldn't say so.
Anne	I know almost for certain that Margot would never kiss anyone unless she was engaged to them. And I'm sure too that Mother never touched a man before Pim.* But I don't know…things are so different now…What do you think? Do you think a girl shouldn't kiss anyone except if she's engaged or something? It's so hard to try to think what to do, when here we are with the whole world falling around our ears and you think…well…you don't know what's going to happen tomorrow and… What do you think?
Peter	I suppose it would depend on the girl. Some girls, anything they do's wrong. But others…well…it wouldn't necessarily be wrong with them. *(The carillon starts to strikes nine o'clock.)* I've always thought that when two people…
Anne	Nine o'clock. I have to go.

---

* Pim is Anne's nickname for her Father.

Peter	That's right.
Anne	*(Without moving)* Goodnight. (*Their faces are close together. There is a second's pause. Then Peter, too shy to kiss her, moves upstage.*)
Peter	You won't let them stop you from coming?
Anne	No. *(She rises and starts for the door, then turns back to him.)* Some time I might bring my diary. There are so many things in it that I want to talk over with you. There's alot about you.
Peter	What kind of thing?
Anne	I wouldn't want you to see some of it. I thought you were a nothing, just the way you thought about me.
Peter	Did you change your mind, the way I changed my mind about you?
Anne	Well—you'll see…

(For a second Anne stands looking up at Peter, longing for him to kiss her. As he makes no move she turns to go. Then suddenly he grabs her arm and turning her around, holds her awkwardly in his arms, kissing her on the cheek. Anne floats out slowly, dazed. She stands for a moment…shutting the door of his room after her…)

JOSH AND S.A.M.
SCREENPLAY BY FRANK DEESE

In the movie, *Josh and S.A.M.*, two brothers run away from home after they are led to believe that they have accidentally killed a man. On their journey, they meet an eccentric young woman who facilitates their get-away by driving their stolen car and pretending to be their baby sitter for the sake of public appearance. During the course of their adventure together, Josh and Sam learn the importance of sticking together against all odds.

Josh and Sam's parents are divorced, and normally Josh and Sam live with their Mom, and their Mom's French boyfriend, *"J.P."* When the summer rolls around, however, it's time once again for Josh and Sam to go to Florida, where they stay with their father, their father's second wife *and* their aggressively athletic step-brothers, *Curtis* and *Leon*. Because Sam is athletic, he is accepted by this side of the family; but Josh, who is more brain than brawn, is tormented by his macho step-brothers, and ignored by his own father. Josh and Sam haven't gotten along too well recently, either, so this puts Josh in the lonely position of being the family outcast. The situation gets worse and worse for Josh until finally he can't stand it anymore. In an attempt to create one ally in the family, Josh comes up with a bizarre plan.

In the following scene, Josh puts his strategy into action. Using a computer, some paper, and a lot of imagination, Josh gets Sam to believe the wildest of stories.

2 Boys
Josh (age 12) and Sam (age 8)

Josh	You know, Sam, I didn't want to mention this with Mom around but I know where's there's this secret place where all the kids like you who fail a grade get together. It's right on the bluffs, high above the Pacific Coast Highway.
Sam	What do they do there?
Josh	Jump off.
(A moment)	

Sam	You're not my brother any more.
Josh	What?
Sam	I just decided it. The same way Dad isn't Mom's husband anymore.
Josh	You must be dumber than Dad's stepsons! You can't divorce me!

Sam	Uh huh, Dad could take you away forever, like he took the lawnmower and the barbecue.
Josh	That wouldn't matter. I'd still be your brother, wherever I was. Even if I was a thousand million miles away.
Sam	Not any more you're not.
Josh	Say it all you want, Sam, you can't change who your brother is. Or even your parents. You're just stuck with whatever you get. *Forever.*
Sam	Na ah, when I get to Florida, I'm making Curtis and Leon my real brothers…'cause they don't like you *either.*

Josh	I don't care. And it doesn't matter either.
Sam	How come?
Josh	'Cause I just discovered something really bad that I have to tell you about. *(Sam starts to leave.)* This is *real.* I found something serious on Dad's computer last night. Something he's been keeping a secret all this time.
Sam	So?
Josh	It's about you.
Sam	Is not. *(Thinks)*
Josh	Yeah… You know. You're probably right. *(Josh turns to walk away. Sam calls after him.)*
Sam	What is it?

Josh   It's the real reason why you're having trouble at school. And why you're always fighting with kids at recess and getting into trouble…and even why you're so good at football…

Sam   *(Seems skeptical, but at the same time intrigued.)* Why?

(Josh motions Sam to follow him to the side of the house.)

Sam   C'mon, Josh. Why is that?

Josh   *(Josh swallows hard. He musters a more intense expression, he's so upset to repeat this.)* I found proof on Dad's computer that you were genetically engineered and secretly trained to be a fighter, a soldier, a *child-warrior.*

Sam   *(Studies Josh's sincere face, totally confused)* You're making this up.

Josh   I'm not! Why do you think they're always calling you "S.A.M."?

Sam   It's my name!

Josh   No! It's your acronym. *(Josh unfolds a paper from his pocket looking very official with "S.A.M." printed in big letters across the top.)* It stands for "**Strategically Altered Mutant.**"

(Sam looks at the paper and Josh with his mouth open.)

Josh   Listen, I have more proof than this. I tossed some secret documents out this morning. I'll watch out for Dad and you look under the window of his office. Go on. Get 'em.

(Sam exits and returns a few moments later with more "documents.")

Josh   Go ahead. Read it for yourself.

Sam   *(Reading)* 'Dear Secretary of Defense'...What's that?

Josh   He's the guy who runs the Pentagon; the head of all the Army.

Sam   Oh. *(Reading slow)* 'Regarding the Killer S-A-M, Strat-e-gi-cally Altered Mutant;' *(He pauses and swallows hard as Josh takes over reading the letter.)*

Josh   *(Reading)* 'Please note that the funds for his delivery are to be split between myself and his gestating unit.' *(To Sam)* That means Mom. *(Reading again)* 'We believe our 'Killer Sam' will be a fine soldier, programmed to fight, kill, and give up his life for your cause. If you ever have need for another one, please let us know. It has been a pleasure doing business with you. Sincerely, Thomas Whitney.'

(Josh watches carefully for Sam's reaction, which is simply a blank face.)

Sam   *(Rubs gently over the type on the page and his father's signature as if to feel if they're real.)* Dad wrote this?

Josh   I didn't see him, but it's his signature. I found these in a secret file on the computer.

(Josh shows the stunned Sam the other pages.)

Sam   *(Seeing his photo on one of the pages.)* This is me.

Josh   *(Pointing to the "document.")* This here shows how you were genetically altered to be a fighter. This describes your enhanced tactical mental powers for war strategy.

Sam   But... I failed second grade.

Josh   Only 'cause you can't learn like normal kids. You absorb information only through special numbers and coded words.

(Sam thinks it all through, dumbfounded and astounded.)

Josh   And look here. This is a diagram of the electronic aiming device inside your right eye. It's why you're so good at sports. 'Cause you were made to be that way. And you know that scar on your forehead Mom and Dad said was from you falling out of the crib?

(Sam feels it on his head while he looks at the pages.)

Josh   That's where they inserted the microchip computer! *(Reading)* 'To control and track movement of the mutant child on the battlefield.'

(Sam stands there, shocked and overwhelmed.)

Sam   Josh. Why didn't they tell me?

Josh   Because they were only thinking of themselves. When they deliver you to the Pentagon, Mom's going to use the money to go off to Europe with J.P. And get this—Dad's sending you off to fight in a war just so he can send the buttholes to *football camp!*

(Sam finally blows up in anger and tears.)

Sam   Josh, I don't want to fight! I don't want to go to war!

Josh   *(A bit overwhelmed by what he's done.)* Don't worry. You won't. It's a good thing I found this out in time, because I'm not going to let it happen. But you know what? We have to keep this quiet and we have to stick together. No more teaming up with Dad's stepsons 'cause they're in on it, too. All their sports stuff is just training you for the battlefield.

(Josh folds up the papers and puts them in his pocket.)

Josh   C'mon. We better get back. *(He leads the frightened, angry and confused Sam back toward the house.)*

Sam   Josh! There was a kid in my class also named Sam. Was he one too?

Josh   Coulda been. The Pentagon documents did mention some others.

Sam   Then we gotta warn them. We gotta save them too.

Josh   We gotta keep quiet. That's all we gotta do for now.

Sam   How can you say you don't want to talk about it?

Josh   What can you do, Sam, it sucks.

Sam   *(Thinks)* I can tell Mom I know the truth. I can show her the documents.

Josh   No! If she sees 'em she'll destroy 'em. Then she'll say I made it all up.

Sam   Then what am I going to do? What do the other Killer Sams do? *(Josh looks into Sam's frightened and expectant face.)* Come on, Josh. Please. You gotta help me.

(Josh thinks hard.)

Josh	Yeah, well, I didn't want to tell you this 'cause I didn't want to get your hopes up. But I read on the computer about the others escaping on something they call the "UNDERGROUND ROADWAY."
Sam	You mean like a big, long tunnel?
Josh	No. They just called it that 'cause it's a secret escape network, you know, that uses back roads with special drivers so the Army won't catch them. Then at night they form big caravans of Mutant Child Warriors all moving north.
Sam	To where?

(Josh hesitates, thinking)

Josh	To Canada. Just like the soldiers who didn't want to fight in Vietnam.
Sam	I know where that is! I can go there, too!
Josh	No, not alone. Not without finding the supreme commander first… She's probably leading a new group to safety and freedom right now.
Sam	Their commander, she's a girl?
Josh	A woman. A great woman. But really just a normal woman who's great because she cares so much about these children who've been made into soldiers that she raids their homes at midnight, takes them away, then protects them all the way to their new homes in Canada.
Sam	I gotta find her, Josh.
Josh	I don't know how.
Sam	What's she look like?

Josh   I don't know. I never saw a picture of her. *(Glancing down, Josh spies the light-haired girl on the small "SPARKLE MAID" juice box.)* But the computer described her as having long, wavy blond hair. And real beautiful-looking. And she wears a red hat when she's out on her mission leading Mutant children north to Canada. They don't know her name except that's she's called "Liberty." *(Glancing at juice box)* The "Liberty Maid." That's what they call her. But you'll never find her. Just asking would give you away.

Sam   Why didn't she come and get me, too?

Josh   *(Looks at Sam, genuinely hurt by not being taken.)* I don't know. Maybe it's not your time yet. Maybe you're still safe.

Sam   What else did you find out?

Josh   I don't think it's a good idea to talk here because I think it's bugged.

Sam   Josh, I have to know everything!

Josh   *(Somber)* Africa.

Sam   What's going on in Africa?

Josh   A war. A secret and brutal war that they want *you* to fight in.

Sam   That's not fair! They can't do that!

Josh   I know they can't, 'cause I'm not going to let 'em. Listen, I'm going to go and see if I can find a driver for the underground roadway. It might take a couple of hours or more so don't open the door for anyone; and don't tell anyone where I am, okay?

Sam   Why can't I go with you?

Josh   'Cause, there could be scouts from the Pentagon out there. And they know what a Killer Sam looks like. So don't go anywhere, or do anything till I come back.

(As Josh sticks his head out to look down the hallway, he turns to Sam with a super serious face. He gives him a thumbs-up, then disappears out the door.)

Josh   So long, Killer Sam.

THE LEMON SISTERS
SCREENPLAY BY JEREMY PIKSER

Set in Atlantic City, New Jersey, the film *The Lemon Sisters* is the story of the friendship between three girls, Franki, Eloise and Nola. The film follows their lives as they each experience success and failure; love and loss. Throughout it all, the one thing that remains the same is the love and loyalty that the three friends share with one another.

Surrounded by the flashy, glittery nightlife of Atlantic City, the girls dream of becoming glamourous, famous nightclub singers! Franki is obsessed with the idea of becoming a star. Eloise lives alone with her father, an eccentric widower who collects show business memorabilia for a living. Nola's family owns a local candy store on the Atlantic City boardwalk.

The following scene takes place on the beach under the boardwalk at night, as the girls make their secret pact to be best friends forever. They swear upon three lemons, prizes that they won that day at the fair.

3 Girls
Nola, Eloise and Franki (all age 9)

Three girls, Nola, Eloise and Franki enter running. They are on the beach in Atlantic City under the boardwalk on a warm summer's night. They are very excited and there is an air of conspiracy and secrecy among them.

Nola   C'mon Franki!

Franki   Coming!

Eloise   Who has the candles?

Franki   I have the candles!

Nola   Hurry!

Franki   Hey, my legs are too short.

Nola   Do you have the table cloth?

Eloise   Here it is. Take this other end.

(Nola and Eloise each take an end of the cloth and drape it over the crate. Franki comes in running. She carries a little purse from the 1950's, which contains three lemons, and a candle. The three girls get settled around their make-shift table, an old crate or box covered with a velvety cloth. They set the candle in the middle. The lemons are spilled on the table and each girl grabs one and puts a lemon in front of her.)

Nola   Okay, everyone, put your hand on your lemons. "With this secret I do swear…"

Franki & Eloise "With this secret I do swear…"

Franki   "…Cross my heart and hope to die, stick a needle in my eye…"

Nola & Eloise "…Cross my heart and hope to die, stick a needle in my eye…"

Eloise	"...Pull out my teeth...and stick 'em up my nose!"
Franki & Nola	"...Pull out my teeth...and stick 'em up my nose!"
Nola	...that the lemon sisters will stay together...and be best friends...and meet every Monday, for eighty-three million, four hundred and fifty-two thousand, two hundred and seventeen years...
Franki & Eloise	*(Overlapping Nola, as they struggle to repeat her.)* "...for eighty three million, four hundred and fifty-two thousand, two hundred and seventeen years..."
Nola	And four months.
Franki & Eloise	And four months.
Franki	Amen.
Nola & Eloise	Amen.

Franki	And then we'll grow up, and become famous singers. The "Lovely Lemon Sisters!"
Eloise	And sing in all the casinos on the boardwalk.
Nola	Everyone in Atlantic City will know us.
Eloise	And give us free popcorn and cotton candy!
Franki	What about costumes? Singers always have beautiful costumes.
Nola	Well...I guess we *could* wear matching outfits.
Franki	But *I* think *I* should wear gloves.
Eloise	Yeah. And capes.

Nola Capes? What for?

Eloise I don't know. They're neat.

Franki Look. I have something special to show you guys. *(Pulling a little bottle of cream from out of her purse. The other girls look at it intently.)* I took it from my Aunt Rose. *Really*. It's supposed to make your *bosoms* grow.

Nola How does it work?

Franki I don't know.

Eloise Let's just put it on.

Nola No, El. What if you put on too much?

Eloise So?

Nola So…you'll look pretty stupid with giant bosoms.

Eloise I look pretty stupid with *no* bosoms.

Franki *(Excited)* So, just put it on!

Nola Well, wait a minute. *(To Franki)* How big are your Aunt Rose's?

Franki *(Proudly)* Pretty big.

Nola Okay, try it.

(Eloise starts to take some cream from the jar. Then she stops and looks at the cream on her hand.)

Eloise I wonder if it makes your hand grow.

Nola Better not do it.

Franki	Well, we have to do *something* to initiate ourselves as official lemon sisters.
Nola	I know.
Eloise	What?
Nola	We can tell our deepest secret.
Eloise & Franki	Okay!
Franki	Who goes first?
Nola	Well, I guess I should. My secret is…I don't have a secret.
Franki	You do, too!
Nola	No, I don't.
Eloise	Well, what's the worst thing you ever did?
Nola	I killed a turtle.
Franki	What???!!!
Nola	I didn't mean to. I guess I just forgot to feed it, and it died.
Eloise	Okay. You go Frank.
Franki	Okay…My secret is…one time I saw my Mom and Dad *naked*.
Nola	You did?
Eloise	Were they…*doing* anything?
Franki	Yeah. They were getting dressed.
Eloise & Nola	Oooooh….
Eloise	…*Good* one Frank.

Nola	Come on Eloiser, your turn.
Eloise	My secret is…my Dad cries.
Nola	*Your* Dad?
Franki	Why?
Eloise	I don't know. The first time I saw him I asked him. He said "Nothing's wrong, go back to bed." That's the meanest he's ever been to me.
Nola	Does he cry all the time?
Eloise	No…just once in a while. I go and watch him until he stops. Then I go back to bed.
Nola	I'm sorry, El.
Franki	Me too.
Eloise	It's okay. He'll be alright. I'll take good care of him.

(They pause for a little while, each in their own thoughts.)

Franki	What if I never moved here?
Nola	We wouldn't be friends.
Franki	You and Eloise would be friends.
Nola	Yeah, but it would be different.
Eloise	Yeah. Three is better than two. My Dad says, that's why the pyramids have three sides…three is *magic*.

(The three girls put their lemons in the center of the table and pile their hands on top of each other on top of the lemons. Lights fade as they all hold hands. They are bonded for life.)

A LITTLE ROMANCE
SCREENPLAY BY ALLAN BURNS
BASED ON THE NOVEL
"E2MC2 MON AMOUR" BY PATRICK CAUVIN

The film *A Little Romance* depicts the story of a French boy, Daniel, and an American girl, Lauren, who meet one day on a film set in Paris and become girlfriend and boyfriend. Both are 12 years old.

When Daniel and Lauren first meet, Lauren is sitting alone unhappily in the corner of the film set. Her mother, who insisted that Lauren come along, has just abandoned her in order to flirt shamelessly with the film's director. Disgusted with the whole thing, Lauren buries herself in a book.

Right before the following excerpt begins, Daniel has managed to sneak, uninvited, onto the film set so he can watch the movie being made. He is practically an expert on films, since he has seen so many. In fact, he has taught himself English just from watching so many American films!

When he spots Lauren sitting alone, however, his interest changes rapidly from watching the actors to meeting this pretty new girl. As they slowly get to know one another, Daniel and Lauren are to discover that, although they come from separate countries and from very different backgrounds, they have more in common with one another than with anyone else they have ever met before.

Special Notes
The following excerpts can be performed in sequence, with short black-outs in between to indicate the passage of time.

1 Boy and 1 Girl
Daniel and Lauren (both age 12)

In this first scene, Daniel, sneaking around on the film set, sees Lauren for the first time. When he hears the make-up man on the film set call her by name, he takes this opening as an opportunity to meet her.

(Daniel sneaks into the filming area, hiding behind a make-up table. As he does, he passes Lauren, a girl of about his age, who is sitting in a chair a few feet away, reading a book, completely oblivious to the activity around her. Her face is hidden in the book.)

The Make-up Man *(From offstage)* Having a good time, Lauren?

(Lauren looks up, nods vaguely, then goes back to her book. Daniel sees Lauren for the first time, and moves slightly closer, watching her reading. He stands on tiptoe to try to see what book could interest her more than the making of a movie, but can't make it out.)

Daniel   *(Calls softly)* Lauren?

(She turns and looks in his direction. She is very pretty. Daniel assumes what he believes to be a debonair pose.)

Daniel   Call me Bogey…

Lauren   *(Frowns)* Why?

Daniel   …Because they belong together.

(She looks at him, thoroughly puzzled.)

Daniel   …Lauren and Bogey…Lauren Bacall… Humphrey Bogart…*(As she continues to stare.)* They were married…. Movie stars. She called him Bogey. *(Really sweating now.)* That's why I said to call me Bogey.

Lauren   *(Beat)* Oh.

Daniel   *(Grasping at straws.)* What's that you're reading?

(Lauren quickly closes the book, title down, on her lap)

Lauren   Nothing.

Daniel   Is that your mother? She's very attractive. Is she an actress?

Lauren   No.

(Lauren carefully closes the book again and slips it unobtrusively into a school backpack similar to Daniel's.)

Daniel   I thought maybe you came out here to watch her.

Lauren   No. She came out here to watch *him*.

Daniel   *(Indicating the director.)* George De Marco.

Lauren   You know him?

Daniel   *(Shrugs)* Sure. *"BLOODY TUESDAY"*… *"LIPS"*… *"THE DANDELION TRAIN"*…

Lauren   I don't go to movies much. Is he a good director?

Daniel   He stinks.

Lauren: *(Delighted)* Really?

Daniel   He's the worst.

Lauren   You're not just saying that?

Daniel   The only people who like his movies are two critics in Paris and one, I think, in Pakistan.

(There is a moment here, as Lauren grins at Daniel and he grins back, one of those times that happen only once or twice in a lifetime, where soul mates meet. They savor it for a split second.)

🎎

This next scene between Daniel and Lauren takes place in the gardens of Vaux-Le-Vicomte: Fountains and statues in the magnificently landscapes park-like grounds. The same day. Some time has passed. Daniel sits with Lauren outside of a Chateau in the gardens, some distance from the film crew. Daniel shares his picnic lunch with her. She is ravenously eating a piece of chicken; he is content to watch her as he picks at his food.

Daniel   I didn't know you knew French.

Lauren   I've lived here nearly three years. How come you speak English?

Daniel   School. But movies mostly. I like the American ones.

Lauren   *(Disinterestedly)* Mmm…

Daniel   *(Between bites)* It's beautiful here, no?

Lauren   I think it's awful that places like this were built when so many Frenchmen were starving. *(She finishes off a chicken leg.)* This is fabulous chicken, Bogey. You're lucky to have a mother who can cook like this.

Daniel	I don't have a mother. I make it myself. And my name isn't really Bogey.
Lauren	I thought you said that—
Daniel	That was a joke, you see… Humphrey Bogart was married with Lauren Bacall— *(Looks at her, gives up trying to explain.)* Never mind. My name is Daniel.

(A short, awkward silence, then:)

Lauren	Are you from Paris?
Daniel	Just outside. La Garenne.
Lauren	You live with your father?

(He nods)

Lauren	What does he do?
Daniel	He…sort of….*drives*…
Lauren	A truck?
Daniel	No… a taxi.
Lauren	You shouldn't be embarrassed. It's honest work.
Daniel	Not the way he does it. *(Beat)* You have a father… or just the mother?
Lauren	I have a father. As a matter of fact, I'm on my third.
Daniel	*(Teasing her)* Does your mother divorce them or just kill them?
Lauren	*(Smiles)* They're all still alive.
Daniel	What does the latest one do?

Lauren	Uh…he's in telephones.
Daniel	Telephones… What does he do exactly?
Lauren	*(A deep breath, then)* Well, exactly…he's the head of I.T.T. in Europe. That's—
Daniel	—One of the biggest conglomerates in the world.
Lauren	You've heard of it then.
Daniel	I've also heard of West Germany. *(Beat)* It's not I.T.T., but it's a nice little operation, too.

(She smiles. There is an awkward moment, as he tries to think of something to say.)

Daniel	*(Finally)* So… You're a capitalist?
Lauren	My *father's* a capitalist. My own politics are more…radical than my parents'.
Daniel	It's easy to be liberal when you're rich. I've seen it in films.

♀♀♀♀

Lauren	*(She grimaces in pain)* Ow!
Daniel	Something's the matter with your foot?
Lauren	Just new shoes. They didn't have them in my size, but I liked them.
Daniel	They're very attractive.
Lauren	Thank you.
Daniel	You sure you're all right?
Lauren	Fine.

Daniel   Okay. Then why don't we mosey on down here a
                     piece?

*(They start to walk along in silence for a beat, Lauren trying to hide the
pain of walking, but not very successfully.)*

Daniel   Let me carry your books.

*(He takes it from her and slings it casually over his shoulder, spilling out
half the books in the process. They both stop to pick them up, Daniel terribly
embarrassed.)*

Daniel   I'm sorry, I…

Lauren   That's okay, I do that myself all the time—

(She stops. He has picked up the Heidegger book and looks at it.)

Daniel   *(Shocked, holding up the book.)* Heidegger?

Lauren   *(Quickly)* It's for school. An assignment.

Daniel   They assign you *Heidegger?!*

Lauren   *(Grabbing book and stuffing it in bag.)* Sure.

Daniel   They are teaching you *Existentialism?!!*

(Lauren is non-plussed; She's never gotten this response before.)

Lauren   *(Tentatively)* Heidegger isn't really an Existentialist.

Daniel   He *claims* he isn't. His writing says he is.

Lauren   *(Testing) You* read *Heidegger?*

Daniel   Not any more. He bores me. Especially his fasci-
                     nation with that old German poet…what's his
                     name…

Lauren   Hölderlin!

Daniel	Hölderlin! Did you ever try to struggle through any of that stuff—like *"The Death Of Empedocles"?*
Lauren	Empedocles!! It's just *awful!* But the French translation is terrible.
Daniel	Believe me, it's terrible in *any* language.
Lauren	I know! I know! *(She is amazed at what they have in common.)* That's fantastic!

(A moment)

Lauren	What's your IQ?
Daniel	I don't know.
Lauren	You mean you've never been tested?

(He shakes his head.)

Lauren	Why not?
Daniel	I'm afraid they might find out that I'm…
Lauren	What?
Daniel	*(Shrugs)* …A genius or something weird. *(She looks at him)* Well, people don't exactly love smart kids.
Lauren	I know. *(Then, a confession)* I'm 167 IQ…
Daniel	I won't tell anybody.
Lauren	…and I read Heidegger because I want to. Not for school. I was lying.
Daniel	I lie all the time. You have to.
Lauren	Are you good at math?
Daniel	Math? I'm sensational. Especially things like

probability. I've won eight hundred and fifty thousand francs on the horses this year!

Lauren   *850.000??!!*

Daniel   Just on paper, naturally...

Lauren   That's fantastic!

Daniel   Fantastique!

Lauren   Fabulous!

Daniel   Formidable!

Adult voice   Hey, Kid! Your mother's got half the crew
from offstage   looking for you! C'mon!

Lauren   *(to Daniel)* I have to go.

Daniel   *(Reluctantly)* Me, too.

(They stand there, neither moving.)

Lauren   Thanks for the lunch.

Daniel   My pleasure.

(Anther beat, as neither moves to go.)

Lauren   Au'voir, Danielle.

Daniel   Au'voir, Lauren.

(She starts to go, then turns back. The following exchange goes very rapidly.)

Lauren   We can meet somewhere—in Paris.

Daniel   When?

Lauren   *(Thinks)* Next week?

Daniel	When next week?
Lauren	*(Thinks again)* Monday!
Daniel	Okay.
Lauren	Where?
Daniel	Where do you live?
Lauren	Neuilly. *(pronounced Nu-Yee)*
Daniel	I'll see you at the Gare Saint Lazare—the train station! Three o' clock.
Lauren	*(Ever romantic)* Under the clock!

(She waves and she's gone, leaving Daniel slightly dazed.)

♀♀♀♀

In the following short excerpt, several days have passed and Daniel and Lauren are out on a date with one another. They are clearly amazed that they have found one another.

Lauren	I used to think...maybe a long time ago... like...like in the time of the *pharaohs* or Louis the thirteenth...that there was somebody made just perfect for me. I mean, when you think about it...assuming that your feelings of love begin when you're about ten...and if you live to say, seventy...well that's pretty limiting because what chance is there that he'll be alive at the same time you are, you know?
Daniel	I thought the same thing. I mean, even if she lived in my lifetime, what if my perfect woman lived in India, or California...or *Brazil?* What chance is there that I meet her...when I live in La Garenne?

Lauren   It's incredible, isn't it?

(They look at one another.)

Daniel   Absolutely. Incredible.

(Blackout.)

LOOKING FOR CORKY JOHNSON
ADAPTED BY
WILLIAM BALZAC
FROM THE SCENE "KRISTIN & JANICE"
BY RUTH MAE RODDY

Two girls hide in the bushes and spy on a group of boys, only to find out that what one finds handsome, the other thinks is funny-looking. But looks aren't everything when it comes to love…

2 Girls
Kristin and Janice

Two girls run into a park and hide behind some bushes. They are spying on some boys.

Kristin	Quick, this way! Behind this fence! There they are!
Janice	A hunk a hunk a hunk a!
Kristin	Sh! Quiet! They'll hear you.
Janice	Don't be a dweeb.
Kristin	Oh, there's Corky Johnson!
Janice	Where?
Kristin	Over there, kicking the soccer ball.
Janice	Corky Johnson? Oooooh! He isn't cute, he's gross.
Kristin	He is not.

Janice	Look there's Eddie Clark! He is *so* cute. Megalie cute!
Kristin	No way. He's got these ears that stick way out and make him look like a donkey.
Janice	He does not. He has nice ears. And good manners. He opened the door for me one time.
Kristin	Every time I look at him I almost laugh.
Janice	That's not nice. Making fun of people isn't nice.
Kristin	But he looks like Dumbo. *(She pulls out her ears.)*
Janice	Stop that! You don't see me making fun of Corky Johnson even though he's got a neck that's too long. *(She extends her neck.)*
Kristin	I thought you said it wasn't nice to make fun of people.
Janice	Can I help it if his neck is funny?
Kristin	*(Staring at Corky Johnson)* He's really cute.
Janice	*(Staring at Eddie Clark)* He's perfect.
Kristin	He's too tall to be perfect.
Janice	But he's really cute.
Kristin	You love him. I'm gonna go tell him.
Janice	No!
Kristin	Ok, *you* go tell him, or I will.
Janice	I can't!
Kristin	You're being a dweeb.

Janice	I don't want anyone to know. Promise me you won't tell, promise?
Kristin	I won't tell if you won't tell about Corky.
Janice	I won't, I promise. If you won't tell about Eddie.
Kristin	It'll be our secret.
Janice	Forever?
Kristin	Forever.

(Pause. They watch the boys for a few moments. They sigh.)

Kristin	You really don't think Corky Johnson is cute?
Janice	His glasses are so thick they make his eyes look like a fish's. And his clothes are awful. Why do you like him?
Kristin	He's funny, he makes me laugh and he's nice.
Janice	Eddie makes me laugh too, even if his ears look like Dumbo.
Kristin	Sometimes it's hard to know when people are cute.
Janice	Maybe being cute isn't everything.
Kristin	Yeah.
Janice	Yeah.

(Lights out)

MY GIRL
SCREENPLAY BY
LAURICE ELEHWANY

The film *My Girl* portrays the story of Vada *(pronounced Vay-da),* an eleven year old girl, and her friendship with her neighbor, Thomas Jay. Vada lives in Pennsylvania with her father and grandmother. Her mother died when she was born. Vada's father works as an undertaker, and so the house in which they live is part home, part funeral-home.

Vada's father needs to hire a make-up artist for the corpses at the funeral home. When an attractive young woman arrives at the house one day in response to his "Help Wanted" ad, sparks fly! It looks as though Vada's father is in love for the first time since the death of Vada's mother. This brings up many questions for Vada, not only in terms of what it means to have her mother replaced, but also about the strange nature of love.

In the following excerpt, Vada and Thomas Jay are sitting by the shores of a beautiful lake.

1 Girl and 1 Boy
Vada and Thomas Jay (both age 11)

Vada Why do you think people want to get married?

Thomas Jay Well, when you get older you just have to.

Vada I'm going to marry Mr. Bixler.

Thomas Jay You can't marry a teacher. It's against the law.

Vada It is not.

Thomas Jay Yes it is, cause then he'll give you all A's and it won't be fair.

Vada That's not true. *(Pause)* Did you ever kiss anyone?

Thomas Jay Like they do on TV?

Vada Mm hm.

Thomas Jay No.

Vada Maybe we should. Just to see what's the big deal.

Thomas Jay But I don't know how.

Vada Here practice on your arm, like this *(She kisses up and down her arm.)*

Thomas Jay Like this? *(He kisses his arm like Vada.)*

Vada Mm hmm. *(They kiss their own arms for a little while.)* OK, enough practice. Close your eyes.

Thomas Jay Then I won't be able to see anything.

Vada Do it.

Thomas Jay Okay, okay!

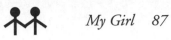

Vada	Okay, on the count of threee: one…two…two and a half…*three.*
(They kiss.)	
Vada	Say something. It's too quiet.
Thomas Jay	Um…um…
Vada	Just hurry!
Thomas Jay	I pledge allegiance to the flag of The United States Of America…
Both	…And to the Republic for which it stands one nation under God, indivisible, with liberty and justice for all.
Vada	Better not tell anyone.
Thomas Jay	You better not either.
Vada	Let's spit on it.
Thomas Jay	OK.
(They spit.)	
Vada	See you tomorrow.
Thomas Jay	OK. See you. *(He walks a little ways and then stops and calls back to her.)* Vada.
Vada	What?
Thomas Jay	Would you think of me?
Vada	For what?
Thomas Jay	Well…If you don't get to marry Mr. Bixler.
Vada	I guess.

NIGHT TRAIN TO BOLINA
BY NILO CRUZ

The play, *Night Train to Bolina* by Nilo Cruz, tells the story of two friends, Clara (age 12) and Mateo (age 11), who run away from home in order to escape their difficult lives in a rural Latin American village.

Clara and Mateo's close friendship is based on many shared painful experiences...the absence of love at home, extreme hunger and deprivation as a result of a series of natural disasters in their farming community, and—worst of all—the oppressive presence of warfare in Latin America.

Mateo believes the only way to survive is to escape to the city, and he convinces Clara to go with him. According to plan, they stow away in boxes on the Night Train, and secretly leave home forever. Once they arrive in the city, however, they face many hardships of a different kind. In the city, Clara and

Mateo have no place to live, no money, no family or friends. In addition, a wound to Mateo's hand has become dangerously infected. With nowhere else to go, the two children sleep on the steps of a church. When they are discovered by a man from the church, Clara and Mateo are eventually brought to a mission, where, sadly, the two friends are separated at the time when they need each other the most. In a world which forces them apart, Clara and Mateo must struggle to find the way back to one another.

Scene 1
1 Girl and 1 Boy
Clara (age 12) and Mateo (age 11)

The following scene takes place with Clara and Mateo still in their village, but just about to begin their long journey to the city. Moments before the scene begins, they write a letter to God, expressing their need to leave home, and asking for God's protection. They go to the cemetery, where Mateo keeps his kite hidden, and tie the note to the kite's string, flying the message as high as it will go. When the scene opens, the kite is in the air, and the two children are watching it carry their wish upwards into the skies.

"THE NIGHT TRAIN"

Soft Music. In the cemetery. On the scrim a photograph of a cemetery is projected. Mateo flies his kite. The kite is suspended in midair. Clara stands close to him with two large boxes.

Mateo   Look at it fly… That's how we're going to be, free….Free….We're going to be free when we escape.

(Waves his kite)

Clara   Let him go…Break the string.

Mateo   No, let him fly higher.

Clara   Just let him go.

(Mateo cuts the string with his teeth. The kite disappears. They wave to the kite in silence.)

Mateo	Now he can fly and take the message, then he can go to die where he belongs.
Clara	I want to go to my house.
Mateo	You can't go back, and neither can I. I can't go back. I told you my sister Flora heard me talk in my sleep last night. She heard me talk about our escape. That's why Mama tied my leg to the kitchen table, 'cause Flora told Ma I was talking in my sleep about going to the city. I cut the rope with my teeth. Ha! They thought I couldn't get away.
Clara	I want to go home, Mateo. I'm afraid.
Mateo	You can't go home anymore. Let's go play with the dead people.
Clara	No, I don't want to play.
Mateo	This is going to be the last time we play with them, then they'll never see us again. Come on! Let's play pretend. I'll be the man who died in October. You be the woman who died in July. You remember the photograph on her tomb? Let's go look for her.
Clara	No.
Mateo	You don't like her? You can be another dead woman, if you want. How about the woman who died in 1949? You remember the picture on her tomb? What was her name?
Clara	Rita.
Mateo	Come on….You pretend to be Rita. I'll pretend to be the man who died in October. *(Reaches for her hand.)* Come on let's go look for their tombs.

Clara	I want to go home.
Mateo	You can't go home, Clara. You can't go home. If you go to your house, they'll tie your leg to a table, then you won't be able to escape.
Clara	I'm not going to the city, Mateo. I want to wait. We can leave when it's meant for us to leave. When God thinks it's meant for us to go.
Mateo	Why are you saying that?
Clara	'Cause we shouldn't go.
Mateo	Why not? I thought we had it all planned. Look at me, we jump on the train. I get in this box. You get inside the other box. No one will see us. *(Gets inside the box.)*
Clara	I promised to be good.
Mateo	I'll leave alone. And when I leave, you'll never see me again. I'll never come back. I'll never come back, you hear me! I thought we had it all planned.
Clara	I'm afraid. In the city there are soldiers. They'll take us away. *(There are tears in her eyes.)*
Mateo	Nothing's going to happen. When the night train comes, we jump on it. We get on and nothing will happen. I know which wagon to get on. The one with the luggage. We hide in the boxes…Come on….
Clara	No. I promised to be good.
Mateo	In the city we can sell cigarettes. Like my brother Luis. Five cents each. I know how to do it. We'll make money. And I will buy you a little rug with

the money I make. And you can sell fruits and beans on the sidewalk. When I make more money, we can get a table. Like the ones in the market, and we can put all the merchandise on top of the table, like real vendors.

Clara   And where are we going to live?

Mateo   Anywhere.

Clara   No, I can't.

Mateo   We could live on the church steps. I've seen people living there.

Clara   I can't go. I made a promise to be good.

Mateo   If you don't come with me I'll die.

Clara   Don't say that.

Mateo   All of me will break into little pieces. And I'll be dead. Dead! Watch…I'll stop breathing. *(Covers his mouth.)*

Clara   Don't do that! Stop it!……………… *(Mateo continues to hold his breath. He runs away from her. She runs after him.)* Stop it…. You're scaring me…. Stop it Mateo.

Mateo   If you don't come with me, I'll die…
If you don't come with me, I'll die…

(He runs faster around the stage)

Clara   Stop it! You're going to get sick…*(Mateo falls to the ground. He pretends to be dead.)* Mateo… Mateo…

(There is a pause.)

Clara	Wake up….Don't play dead….I know you're not dead. *(Mateo doesn't respond.)* Mateo….Oh God! Wake up, Mateo! *(There are tears in her eyes)* Mateo…. Please wake up…. Wake up!!!! Wake up…. I'll go with you…. I promise to go with you…. Please wake up…. I promise…

(Mateo opens his eyes)

Clara	You scared me…
Mateo	You promise to go with me?
Clara	Yes…. Yes…. I'll go with you.
Mateo	Tonight.
Clara	Yes.
Mateo	Good. So let's play with the dead people one last time.
Clara	I don't want to play.
Mateo	Come on…. Let's play…. I'm the dead man who died in October. My name is Faro. My tomb is right there.
Clara	I'm the dead woman who died in July.
Mateo	Hello!
Clara	Hello!
Mateo	What's your name?
Clara	Rita. My tomb is back there. My tomb has an angel with a horn. He plays music for me.
Mateo	My tomb has a cross and a wreath of laurel leaves. I was a soldier.

Clara	Soldiers are mean. They kill and steal children.
Mateo	Not me. I was a good soldier.
Clara	All soldiers are bad. I don't talk to soldiers.
Mateo	*(Runs around the stage to look for another tomb.)* All right, then I'll be this man, right here.
Clara	What's your name?
Mateo	I can't read his name. But they call me Pipiolo like my uncle. What's your name?
Clara	I'm still Rita. I'm beautiful like her. I was a singer.
Mateo	I was a barber.
Clara	Would you comb my hair?
Mateo	I lost my comb.
Clara	Well, find your comb and scissors. I'm going to sing tonight and I want my hair combed. See that tomb right there, that's my stage.
Mateo	I'll charge you 25 cents.
Clara	I don't have any money. I can give you the flowers on my tomb.
Mateo	I want 25 cents.
Clara	I don't have any money. The soldiers stoled my money.
Mateo	The soldiers took my comb. Hide. They'll kill you if they find you.

(Both children run around the stage.)

Mateo	Ay! Ay! My hand hurts. —It hurts a lot.

(The game ends)

Clara	Let me look at it. *(She unbinds his bandage.)*
Mateo	Ay!
Clara	Your hand is purple. It's swollen.
Mateo	No, it's not.
Clara	It's infected.
Mateo	It's not infected.
Clara	We have to put something on it. Alcohol.
Mateo	No. Leave it like that. There's nothing wrong with it. Leave it like that.
Clara	Let me wrap it again. *(Bandages his hand.)*
Mateo	In the city you can learn to be a nurse. You could work in a hospital and wear a white uniform.
Clara	Me?
Mateo	Yes. And you can learn to give injections.

(Fade to black.)

Scene 2
2 Girls
Clara (age 12) and Talita (age 14)

Just before this next scene begins, Clara and Mateo have been taken to a mission in the city, where they receive food, shelter and medical care for Mateo's hand. Much to their distress, however, once they arrive at the mission they are separated; Mateo is put in the infirmary, while Clara is placed in a separate room with another girl, Talita. To make matters worse, the nuns at the mission have told Clara that she may not visit, see or speak to Mateo.

Talita, who is two years older than Clara, has lived at the mission for some time now. Her family was destroyed by the war, and now she waits for her adoptive American mother to come and get her.

When the scene opens, it is night time at the mission—Clara's first night apart from Mateo. Upset and anxious, she is unable to go to sleep. Talita, aware of how frightened Clara is, tries to cheer her up and comfort her. In the following scene, Clara and Talita begin to build a friendship which is deeply needed by both.

"A NEW FRIEND AT THE MISSION"

At the mission. There are two beds on the stage. Clara stands to the right of the stage. Talita lies in bed to the left of the stage.

Talita   When the little stick points to seven and the big stick points to twelve, that's the time the bell rings. That's seven o'clock. That's the time we have to wake up. Sister Nora taught us how to tell time. Have you ever seen a cuckoo clock? It goes cuckoo... cuckoo....And a little bird comes out of the clock. Sister Nora has one in her classroom. Right around this time the bell rings. When the bell rings it's time to go to sleep.

(The bell rings and the lights dim.)

Clara   What happened to the lights?

Talita   It's time to go to sleep. The cuckoo clock must be going cuckoo...cuckoo... Are you afraid? Nothing's going to happen to you. I used to be afraid like you. Natalia, the girl who used to sleep in your bed was afraid too. She was always afraid the roof would cave in at night and soldiers would come in here.

Clara   I want to leave this place. I want to get out.

Talita   You can't. They won't let you.

Clara   Why not?

Talita	Because this is where you belong. Who brought you here? *(Pause.)* Was it your father?
Clara	No.
Talita	Who did?
Clara	A man from the city. He was cleaning the church steps, and I told him my friend was sick. He took us into a little room inside the church. He gave my friend medicine. Then he took us to the hospital in a car. But they didn't want us in the hospital, because there were no beds. So he brought us here, me and my friend. You know where the infirmary is?
Talita	Yes.
Clara	That's where they took my friend. He's sick.
Talita	Was he dying? Did a soldier shoot him?
Clara	No. His hand is infected.
Talita	I clean the floor of the infirmary. I see people die everyday. When I used to live at the Santa Rosa mission I was sick in the infirmary and I saw a boy die next to my bed.
Clara	He's not going to die! Don't say he's going to die!
Talita	Shshshhh…….. They'll hear you outside. We're supposed to be sleeping. —See, I hear someone coming. Someone's coming this way. Go to bed, pretend you're sleeping.

(Sister Nora enters the room. She goes over to Talita's bed and covers her. Then proceeds to Clara's bed and does the same. Sister Nora exits.)

Talita	Run to the door and see if she's gone.

Clara   You do it.

(Talita runs to the door and sees if the nun has left.)

Talita   She'll be back later. She's Sister Nora. She's nice.
When I can't sleep, because I have bad dreams, she
tells me bedtime stories. Except she always falls
asleep instead of me. One time she took us to the
zoo and I saw a monkey called Nunu. He was sitting like this. *(Sits on Clara's bed and crosses her legs.)*
Like a little man with his legs crossed. He wasn't a
boy. He was a woman. Not a woman. A monkey
mother. Her little monkey was sleeping and she
came to me and looked into my eyes, like this.
(Moves her head from side to side.) Then she went
like this with her lips. *(Makes Capuchin monkey
sounds. Does monkey movements and spins around.)*

Clara   *(Laughs)* Do it again.

Talita   Good. I made you laugh. *(Clara becomes serious
again. Talita repeats motions.)* I want you to smile. I
don't want you to be sad. Sister Nora says we have
to share and give to others. I want to bring happiness to your face. Look at me, the little monkey
would put her hand to her nose, like if she was
going to sneeze. Like if she had a cold. Like this.
*(Places her hand on her nose, breathes in and out
through her mouth and spins. Pause. Faces forward.)*
She looked like she wanted to be my mother. I
don't have a mother. I used to have two mothers. I
used to. Not anymore. Now I don't know. One
lived in America and one disappeared from home.
My Papi says she was kidnapped. Do you know
what kidnap means? It means that they steal you.

(Clara shakes her head.)

Talita   The soldiers that come to our village, they come
                          and do bad things. They put people in bags of rice
                          and take them away. Then they throw them into a
                          pit. Were you at the Santa Rosa mission?

(Clara shakes her head.)

                          That's where my father took me, so my American
                          mother can come for me. I'm going to be her
                          daughter. If I show you a secret, promise not to tell
                          anybody.

(Clara nods)

                          Stand there and close your eyes. I don't want anybody
                          to know where I hide my secret. Come on, close
                          your eyes and stand there. Go on over there.

*(Clara closes her eyes and stands apart from Talita. Talita pulls out a bun-
dle from under her bed cushion.)*

                          Open your eyes. And don't tell anybody I showed
                          these.

(Talita takes out a pair of shoes from inside a pillowcase.)

                          My mother sent them to me in a letter. A little
                          box. They didn't fit me when I got them. So my
                          mother gave them to my sister, because she had
                          bigger feet. Now they are small on me, because my
                          feet got big. Try them on. They'll fit you. You have
                          small feet.

(Clara tries them on.)

                          Aren't they beautiful? But you see my sister
                          scratched them. She never took care of them. She
                          was going to break them and get them dirty, so I
                          took them away from her. She was sleeping one

night, and I took them from under the bed. I put them inside a sack, I dug a hole outside the house and buried them, so she wouldn't wear them again. Wait. Let me see if someone's coming.

(She runs to the door and takes a peek. She runs back to Clara.)

The next day everybody in my house was looking for the shoes. And I didn't tell. I didn't say anything. I used to go out at night and dig them out of the ground and wear them for a little while. Even if they were big on me. Then I would polish them with my nightshirt and dab a bit of saliva to make them shine. They would shine so much you could see the bright moon reflected on them. Go see if someone's coming.

(Clara goes to the door.)

Clara   No one's out there.

Talita   Sister Nora will make her round again. Then she'll sit by the door and fall asleep. Let me wear the shoes.

Clara   But they don't fit you.

Talita   It doesn't matter. *(Talita slips her feet halfway into the shoes. She walks around the room flapping them.)*

One night my grandma caught me walking around the garden with the shoes. I said, "Grandma please don't tell. Promise not to tell. Grandma they're mine." And she kept it a secret. Every night I walked out on the moist grass with these shoes. My shoes. And every night I buried them again. I dug them out, when I found out I was going to come here. I put them inside a pillowcase and brought them with me.

(Talita takes off her shoes and places them on her head.)

> One day I will melt them into a hat. My grandma had her gold tooth melted into a ring. I could do the same with my shoes. And I'll have a hat. Maybe a purse.

(Holds them by the strap, as if they were a purse.)

> Maybe a pair of gloves, like the ones rich ladies wear to church.

Clara   Keep them how they are.

Talita   That's true. When I look at them I remember the smell of back home. Walking on the moist grass. The moon shining on my shoes. *(There are tears in her eyes.)*

Clara   You miss your Grandma?

Talita   Sometimes.

Clara   I know my family must go out in the fields everyday looking for me. I can just see them coming home, thinking the wild dogs ate me. I miss Mateo. When will I see him again?

Talita   Pretend you're sick. They'll take you to the infirmary to see a doctor, then you can see him.

(Blackout)

ONE THOUSAND CRANES
BY COLIN THOMAS

The play, *One Thousand Cranes* addresses children's fears and anxieties about nuclear war. *One Thousand Cranes* interweaves the stories of two children living in different nations and at different times, yet whose lives are both profoundly effected by the presence of nuclear weapons. The first story is about Buddy, a twelve-year old Canadian boy, who is obsessed by the possibility of nuclear war in the present day world. The second is the true story of Sadako, a Japanese girl who contracted leukemia nine years after the Hiroshima bombing as a result of the radiation.

When Sadako learned of her illness, she began to fold hundreds of origami paper cranes. According to Japanese legend, a crane will live for one thousand years. By trying to fold one thousand origami cranes, Sadako made a brave attempt to hold on to her life, and to keep her hope of recovery alive.

After Sadako's death, a statue was built in her memory. The statue was of a young girl holding a golden crane, with the inscription "This is our cry. This is our prayer. Peace in the world." Since then, thousands of school children from all over the world have sent origami paper cranes to Sadako's family, in support of world peace.

If you would like to send paper cranes to Hiroshima, the address is:

Ichiro Kawamoto
730 Hiroshima Minami-Ku
Matoba 2-6-4
Kunimitu Biru 303
Hiroshima Orizurunokai
Hiroshima, Japan

Scene 1
2 Girls
Sadako and Yoshiko (both age 12)

In the following excerpt, Sadako plays with her best friend Yoshiko. At this point in the play, Sadako has been suffering from signs of her illness for four months now, but she is afraid to tell her parents, fearful of alarming them.

103

"Too many people get sick in Hiroshima," she says, earlier. In this scene Sadako confides to someone for the first time that she has been feeling ill.

"SKIPPING"

Sadako   *(To the audience)* The only person I ever told was my best friend, Yoshiko.

(Sadako walks forward and grabs a skipping rope, turning to call offstage.)

Yoshiko-chan! Yoshiko-chan! Come out to play!

(Sadako starts to skip by herself. She completes part of the following traditional verse, which may be sung in Japanese, or in its English adaptation, which is presented at the end of the script.)

> *Midori no oka no akai yane*
> *Tongari boshi no tokei dai*
> *Kane ga narimasu "Kin! Kon! Kan!"*
> *Mei-mei koyagi mo naitemasu*
> *Kaze ga soyo-soyo oka no iye*
> *Ki-i-roi omado wa oira no iye yo.* *

(Suddenly dizzy, Sadako stops and leans over, with her hands on her knees. Yoshiko enters. She stands beside Sadako, looking at the ground.)

Yoshiko   Hi, Sadako-chan. Looking for something?

Sadako   Oh, hi, Yoshiko-chan. No.

---

* English adaptation of the Japanese Skipping Song:
The **First Skipping Song,** which Sadako sings by herself, may be adapted as follows:
Red-roofed house that I know
On a grass-green hill.
Clock tower chiming tells the time of day.
The bells in the tower go "Kin Kon Kan."
Wake up little lambs, "Mei, mei, mei."
("Mei" is the sound Japanese lambs make.)

Yoshiko	So, what are you doing? Watching the grass grow?
Sadako	Never mind.

(Sadako looks up, grinning, and the two girls immediately go into a game of "Jan Ken Pon" ["Scissors, Rock, Paper"**] They play several rounds at ever-increasing speed till they can't do it any more. They laugh.)

Sadako	Let's skip.
Yoshiko	Skip?
Sadako	Yeah, skip. You know, with a rope?
Yoshiko	I don't know, Sadako-chan. I just finished my lunch.
Sadako	Lunch? You're always eating, Yoshiko-chan.
Yoshiko	Only because I chew my food very slowly.
Sadako	Right.
Yoshiko	Just let me digest.
Sadako	Okay. *(Sadako sits)* How long?

(Sadako and Yoshiko touch)

Yoshiko	You're sweating. Are you all right? You've been looking a little pale lately.
Sadako	I'm fine.
Yoshiko	Sadako-chan, do you still get dizzy after you run?

** JAN KEN POI

"Jan Ken Pon," or *"Jan Ken Poi,"* as it would be known to girls in Hiroshima, is familiar in the West as "Scissors, Rock, Paper." The chant on the first round is *"Jan ken poi."* If there's a tie, the chant on subsequent rounds is *"Aiko de hoi."*

Sadako	Never. Well, sometimes. Hardly ever, really. It's been four months since field day and I hardly ever get dizzy when I run any more.
Yoshiko	I think you should tell your parents.
Sadako	No. I don't want to scare them. They get so nervous about everything.
Yoshiko	But maybe there's something…
Sadako	Unh unh. Besides, I know I'm getting better.
Yoshiko	How?
Sadako	I know I've got good luck.
Yoshiko	What do you mean?
Sadako	Well, they say it's good luck of you see a spider…
Yoshiko	Yes?
Sadako	Well, I see a spider…right on your neck!

(Yoshiko screams)

Yoshiko	Where? *(Sadako laughs)* Sadako! That's not funny! I practically had a heart attack!
Sadako	*(Still laughing)* I know. I couldn't help it. You were getting so serious.
Yoshiko	Well, it is serious, Sadako.
Sadako	Let's skip it.
Yoshiko	What?
Sadako	Let's skip.
Yoshiko	I don't know, Sadako-chan. I'm still digesting.

Sadako	Okay. You sit. I'll skip.
Yoshiko	Okay. Why don't you do Onami Konami?
Sadako	All right.

(Sadako begins skipping as she and Yoshiko sing. [Please see English version footnoted below.***] Halfway through, Sadako starts to skip pepper.)

Yoshiko & Sadako	*Sora ni saezuru tori no ko-e* *Mine yori otsuru taki no oto* *Onami konami tou-tou to* *Hibiki taesenu umi no oto.* *Kikeya hito-bito omoshiroki* *Kono ten-nen no ongaku o* *Shirabe jizai ni hiki tamau* *Kami no onte no toutoshi ya.*
Yoshiko	No, no. That's not right. You start to spin after you say it.
Sadako	No you don't.
Yoshiko	Yes you do.
Sadako	Okay, Yoshiko-chan, you show me.
Yoshiko	What?
Sadako	You do it.

*** **Onami Konami,** the second song, which the girls sing together, can be simplified and adapted as follows:
Big Wave, small wave,
Waves on the windy days,
Spin right around,
Spin right around.

Yoshiko   Okay. You jump in, okay?

Sadako   Okay.

(Yoshiko begins the verse. Sadako joins in. They skip together.)

Sadako & Yoshiko Sora ni saezuru tori no ko-e... *(They trip.)*

Sadako   How's your digestion?

Yoshiko   My what?

Sadako   *(Poking Yoshiko)* Your tummy.

Yoshiko   *(Giggling)* You jump in again, okay?

Sadako   Okay.

Yoshiko   Okay.

(They skip together again.)

Sadako & Yoshiko Sora ni saezuru tori no ko-e...

(At the end of the verse, they start to skip pepper together. They are both laughing. Suddenly, Sadako stops skipping and stands with her hands on her knees, her feet placed wide apart.)

Yoshiko   What's the matter, Sadako-chan?

Sadako   Nothing...*(Sadako collapses. Yoshiko runs to her.)*

Yoshiko   Sadako-chan!

Sadako   *(Trying to get up)* It...it's nothing. *(She collapses again.)*

Yoshiko   Sadako-chan, are you teasing me?

Sadako   *(Weakly)* No.

Yoshiko   Mrs. Sasaki! Mrs. Sasaki!

(Yoshiko runs off. A siren wails. The transition into the next scene is a swirl of motion…In contrast, the hospital is very still and quiet.)

Scene 2

In this next scene, Sadako is in the hospital and Yoshiko comes to visit her. She brings with her a very special gift.

"CRANES"

(Sadako enters and addresses the audience)

Sadako   In the next few days, the doctors did their tests. When no one was looking, I read the results.

(Yoshiko enters the playing area. She is carrying a furoshiki, which is a cloth-wrapped gift. She calls from outside the door.)

Yoshiko   Sadako-chan! Sadako-chan! Are you awake? It's me, Yoshiko. Hi. *(Yoshiko looks in, then enters Sadako's room. As they do whenever they see one another, the two girls play a quick game of Jan Ken Poi.)* They don't usually allow kids to visit on Thursdays, so I lied at the desk. I told them I was twenty-one. How are you feeling?

Sadako   Fine. They're just doing a few tests.

Yoshiko   I know. Mr. Nomura says you'll be back to school again in no time. You know what we did on Sunday? We all went to Mr. Nomura's house again. Clam-digging. And he boiled sweet potatoes for us to eat. You should have seen Tomiko. She ate four. I was disgusted.

Sadako   How many did you eat?

Yoshiko   Five. Small ones.

Sadako   Yoshiko-chan, you're my best friend, right? Well you've got to tell me the truth. They did the tests

	already. I read the results.
Yoshiko	Sadako!
Sadako	I know I wasn't supposed to, but no one would tell me anything. But there must be some mistake. The tests say I have leukemia from the bomb. That can't be true—?
Yoshiko	Sadako-chan...I....I can't....
Sadako	It's all right. You don't have to say anything, Yoshiko-chan. I know I'll be all right. I don't feel like I'm going to die.
Yoshiko	Oh, Sadako-chan, of course you're not. Mr. Nomura says people don't always die from leukemia...oh.
Sadako	So it is true. *(Sadako turns her face away from Yoshiko.)*
Yoshiko	Oh, Sadako...Sadako-chan, Mr. Nomura says... Mr. Nomura says if anybody can get better from leukemia, you can.
Sadako	Is that true? Did Mr. Nomura really say that?
Yoshiko	Of course it's true. Didn't they tell you?
Sadako	They didn't tell me anything.
Yoshiko	Well, he's our teacher. He ought to know, right? Right? Sadako-chan, what you need is hope. *(Yoshiko unwraps the furoshiki and reveals a large origami crane made out of foil. There are also several pieces of unfolded origami paper.)*
Sadako	What's that?
Yoshiko	A paper crane. He's going to help you get better.

Don't you know the legend of the paper crane?

Sadako   I can't remember.

Yoshiko   Well, cranes are supposed to live for a thousand years, right?

Sadako   Yes.

Yoshiko   Well, the legend says that even if you're very sick, if you fold one thousand paper cranes, the gods will make you better. They'll give you a long life, just like a crane.

Sadako   Oh, Yoshiko-chan, let me see it.

(Yoshiko gives the crane to Sadako.)

Sadako   *(Speaking to the audience)* It was like holding a living bird in my hands. I could almost feel warm feathers and heartbeat. And I could feel my own heartbeat, right down to my toes.

Thank you, Yoshiko-chan.

(Sadako and Yoshiko touch hands. Yoshiko exits. Sadako begins folding her first crane.)

THE REMEMBERER
ADAPTED BY
STEVEN DIETZ
FROM "AS MY SUN NOW SETS"
BY JOYCE SIMMONS CHEEKA
AS TOLD TO
WERDNA PHILLIPS FINLEY

Based on a true story, *The Rememberer* is a play about twelve-year old Joyce, a young Squaxin Indian girl growing up in the Pacific Northwest. In 1911, Joyce was forcibly removed from her family and placed in a government-run boarding school, called the Tulalip Training School. There, Joyce and other Native American students were forbidden to speak their own Native language or practice any of their Native American customs or beliefs. The experience was confusing and often frightening for the students.

But it was particularly difficult for Joyce, who, early in her life, had been named the *"Rememberer"* by her tribe. Without a written language, knowledge among Indian peoples was passed on from generation to generation through stories and recollections. As the chosen Rememberer, Joyce was honored with the responsibility of remembering the history and the ways of her people, and her responsibility as the Rememberer was an important one.

At the Tulalip Training School, Joyce must struggle to hold on to the memory of her heritage, and it isn't easy. Soon it becomes evident to Joyce, through a series of dream-like encounters with her spirit guide, that this painful experience is just another chapter of her people's history that must be remembered for all time.

In the following scene, Joyce and the other girls are in the washroom at the Tulalip Training school. At this point in the play, the girls are buzzing with curiosity about the recent arrival of Darin Longfeather, a rebellious, older student who bears frightening-looking scars on his back.

(Please note that where the girls' lines are in italics, they are speaking to one another in their Native American language.)

113

Scene 1
4 Girls, 2 Women
Joyce (age 12), Girl One (age 15),
Girl Two (age 12), Young Girl (age 8),
Nurse Warner (adult) and Miss Brennan (adult)

(Lights reveal the Washroom, again—as Joyce enters in line behind the other three girls. They bring their tin boxes with them, as before.

Nurse Warner, as before, walks down the line and gives them their tooth powder. They begin to brush their teeth, identically, as before.

Nurse Warner leaves. The girls are alone. They immediately turn and start talking to each other—now brushing any way they want to.)

Girl Two   *You were laughing, I saw you!*

Joyce   *You were laughing louder!*

Young Girl   *Laughing at what?*

Girl Two   *At the fish oil!*

Girl One   *(An urgent whisper) Quiet. She's here—*

(The girls straighten up and brush their teeth very formally, as—Miss Brennan looks in on them.)

Miss Brennan   No Indian words, girls. You know better. *(Miss Brennan checks her hair in the mirror, quickly. She also gives the perfume on her wrist a quick sniff. She smiles.)* I'll see you in class.

(Miss Brennan goes, the girls relax.)

Girl One   You did not!

Girl Two   Yes, I did!

Young Girl   What? Did what?

Girl One   Who saw you?

Girl Two	Joyce saw me.
Young Girl	What? Saw what?
Girl Two	Tell her.
Joyce	Yeah. I saw her.
Girl One	Really?
Joyce	Yeah.
Young Girl	What? Saw her do what?
Girl Two	Tell her, Joyce.
Joyce	She found a bottle of Miss Brennan's perfume.
Girl One	So?
Joyce	And she dumped out the perfume and filled it with fish oil.
Young Girl	Really?
Girl One	*(To Girl Two)* Did she get mad?
Joyce	She hasn't noticed!

(The girls laugh, heartily)

Young Girl	When did you do this?
Girl Two	Two weeks ago!

(The Girls laugh even louder. They finish brushing their teeth and hair during the following.)

Girl One	Darin Longfeather showed me the scars on his back.

(The girls laugh a bit.)

Joyce	What scars?

Girl One	It's not funny. The scars from his other school. Where they whipped him with a belt.

(The girls are more serious now.)

Joyce	Why'd they do that?
Girl One	I don't know. But, they did. I *saw*. That's why he ran away.
Joyce	They caught him and sent him here.
Girl Two	I bet he runs away again.
Girl One	The Sheriff'll kill him if he does. Darin said so.
Joyce	Dr. Buchanan wouldn't let them hurt him.
Girl Two	They can do whatever they want, Joyce. It doesn't matter what the teachers say.
Girl One	Darin said there's no way he'll get caught.
Joyce	What do you mean?
Girl One	He says he knows a secret trail. A secret trail that will get him home.

(A bell rings. The girls file out in a line...)

ᛘᛘᛘᛘ

In this next scene, Joyce talks to the mysterious Darin Longfeather for the first time.

Scene 2
1 Girl and 1 Boy
Joyce (age 12) and Darin Longfeather (teens)

(The school yard. As Joyce walks, she is passed by Darin Longfeather, who is pushing a wheel barrow filled with large feed sacks.)

Joyce stops, as Darin goes past her. When he is nearly gone, she says...)

Joyce   Darin.

(He stops, but does not turn to her. She looks around, then approaches him, cautiously.)

Joyce   I'm Joyce.

(He does not respond.)

Joyce   I've never talked to you.

(He does not respond.)

Joyce   Lillian said at your old school they beat you.

(He turns and looks at her. Long silence.)

Joyce   Why?

Darin   *(Softly)* What did you say?

Joyce   Why? *(Pause)* What did you do?

Darin   You're a stupid girl.

(He grabs the handle of the wheelbarrow and prepares to leave —)

Joyce   *(Angry)* You must have deserved it.

(He immediately lets go of the wheelbarrow and walks up to Joyce. Stands very close to her, frightening her.)

Darin   Do you want to know what I did? DO YOU? *(Pause, softer now)* I said my Mother's name. At night, *in my sleep,* I said my Mother's name. And they heard me. "NO INDIAN NAMES," they said, "NO INDIAN NAMES." So, the next night, they made me sleep on the wood floor, without a blanket. And they watched me. And, I closed my eyes and I tried with all my heart to *forget my Mother's name*. But, in my sleep, I said it again. So, the next night they took me to the barn. And they stuffed cloth in my mouth. And, they all stood around me while I slept. I tried to stay awake. I tried not to think about her, or her face, or her voice. *I tried to pretend my Mother was dead.* But in the middle of the night, they woke me up and tied my hands to a post. They told me I'd said her name again in my sleep. And I swore I'd never do it again—but they said it was too late. That I would have to be taught a lesson. *(Pause)* They took off my shirt. *(Pause)* One of the men took off his belt. *(Pause)* And he started hitting me. *(Pause…)* And I didn't cry. Because I could hear my Mother's voice, saying: *You'll be home soon, my beautiful boy. (Pause, softly)* You'll be home soon.

(Darin stares at Joyce. She says nothing. He walks back to the wheelbarrow. Lifts it.)

Joyce   They say you know a secret trail.

(Darin looks back at her…looks at her for another moment, then pushes the wheelbarrow past…)

THE RISE AND RISE OF DANIEL ROCKET
BY PETER PARNELL

The play *The Rise and Rise of Daniel Rocket* is about a 12-year old boy named Daniel Rocket who discovers that he can fly! Because of his special gift, however, the other children are jealous of him, and he does not fit in at school. Daniel has one best friend named Richard—and a crush on a girl, named Alice, who is in his class at school. All three characters are in the sixth grade.

When the play opens, Daniel is intent on building a mechanical pair of wings for his school science project. He plans on flying as part of his assignment for the science class. But Richard has never seen Daniel actually fly, and he is extremely worried that when Daniel finally *does* try his wings in front of the class that he will crash and hurt himself. What Richard *doesn't* know is that Daniel has been able to fly all his life, ever since he was a baby, and that he doesn't even need the wings. They are just for show.

In the following scene, Richard, concerned for Daniel's safety, tries to persuade him not to attempt to fly for the science project. He goes over to Daniel's house and meets him in the basement where Daniel is building his wings.

Scene 1
2 Boys
Daniel and Richard (both age 12)

Basement. Work area with photographs, diagrams, models, etc. Daniel at work finishing huge wing. Knock at cellar door.

Daniel	Who is it?
Richard	It's me. Daedalus.
Daniel	No. Daedalus was last week.
Richard	Icarus, then.
Daniel	Icarus?
Richard	Son of Daedalus.
Daniel	I know who Icarus was.
Richard	Well…
Daniel	But, he's not the password.
Richard	Come on, Snood, open up!
Daniel	Though he *could* be the password…
Richard	Amelia Earhart.
Daniel	Oh, well, I suppose she'll do. *(Daniel unlocks cellar door. Richard descends.)*
Richard	Who was it?
Daniel	Who?
Richard	Who was the password?
Daniel	Otto von Lilienthal.
Richard	Oh, yeah, I was just reading about him.

Daniel	In that book you're carrying?
Richard	Yes.
Daniel	*Great Air Disasters.* Richard! You're taking an active interest in my work!
Richard	Yes, well. I found him pretty interesting, too.

(Pause)

Daniel	Well, how do you like it?
Richard	It looks great.
Daniel	Will you help me try it on?
Richard	You shouldn't before you've finished it.
Daniel	I can't wait. Will you help me?
Richard	If you want me to. *(Richard helps affix wings to Daniel's shoulders.)* Where does this go?
Daniel	Try under my arm.
Richard	Should I wrap it around?
Daniel	Try under it.
Richard	It *is* under it.
Daniel	It's over it.
Richard	Okay, I'll try under it.
Daniel	Wrap it around.
Richard	I've already wrapped it around.
Daniel	Wrap it around again.
Richard	Okay. Okay.

Daniel	Are you ready?
Richard	Wait, wait. I'm almost through. *(Richard finishes tying Daniel to wings. Stands back. Daniel stands on top of workbench. Flaps his wings slowly. Up and down. Up and down.)* How does it feel?
Daniel	It feels incredible. How does it look?
Richard	It looks incredible.
Daniel	It can't look as incredible as it feels.
Richard	You look like a bird.
Daniel	I feel like a bird.
Richard	That's incredible, Snood.
Daniel	I do! *(Daniel flaps. Richard laughs. Daniel jumps down and "flies" around the basement.)*
Richard	Careful, Snood! You'll break things!
Daniel	I don't care! I don't care!
Richard	Your diagrams! Your plans!
Daniel	I don't care! I'm finished!
Richard	You're *almost* finished!
Daniel	I'm finished! I'm finished!
Richard	Watch the paint! Watch the model!
Daniel	I'm finished! I'm through! *(Daniel slips. Falls in heap on the floor.)*
Richard	Snood! Are you alright?
Daniel	Fine, I'm fine.

Richard	You've got to be careful. You're not yet used to the weight of these things.
Daniel	But I've been practicing all these weeks.
Richard	But it's still not the same.
Daniel	No, it's not.
(Pause)	
Richard	Snood.
Daniel	Yes, Richard?
Richard	I know you've been working hard.
Daniel	Yes.
Richard	And I know you know what you're doing.
Daniel	Mmn.
Richard	But, are you sure, are you completely sure, that it's going to fly?
Daniel	I *told* you it would, Richard...
Richard	Yes, I know, but...
Daniel	I told you to trust me...
Richard	Well, of course I trust you...
Daniel	I'm going to need your help getting out there, and if you're not going to trust me...
Richard	It's just that in this book I've been reading...
Daniel	*Great Air Disasters.*
Richard	Yes...

Daniel	Which you've so suddenly taken an interest in…
Richard	It says that these wings, these—ornithopters— were really the most primitive of fliers. No matter how strong the pilot, no matter how wide the wing span, no matter how good the design. People have tried for centuries—
Daniel	Da Vinci.
Richard	Yes.
Daniel	Lilienthal.
Richard	Yes. Exactly.
Daniel	Wright. Stehling. Von Hauser. Chanute. Langly. Herring.
Richard	Yes, Snood. Yes.
Daniel	I know about them, Richard! I know about them all!
Richard	And none of them succeeded. None of their gliders ever worked. Did they, Snood? *(Pause)* You knew that all along, didn't you?
Daniel	Einstein, Richard.
Richard	Einstein?
Daniel	Where Da Vinci went wrong was in watching the flight of birds. He didn't know about the space/time continuum.
Richard	The space/time continuum?
Daniel	Men can't just build wings—they have to build webs of gravity.
Richard	Webs of gravity?

Daniel   There's a star in space, Richard, that, when I fly, I'll be moving towards. *(Pause)* I'll show you, Richard.

Richard   You'll *show* me?

Daniel   Tomorrow night. If you trust me. If you promise to keep it a secret. Do you promise?

Richard   I…okay. I promise, Snood. *(Pause)*

Daniel   Meet me at Hatch's Cliff tomorrow night.

Richard   Snood! Hatch's Cliff!?!

Daniel   Just trust me, Richard. Trust me. Just meet me there at seven-thirty. *(Richard nods. Turns to leave.)* Oh, and Richard?

Richard   Yes.

Daniel   When you come, bring that stupid girl with you.

Richard   Girl? Which stupid girl?

Daniel   You know. The one in Mrs. Rice's class.

Richard   Judy?

Daniel   No.

Richard   Claudia?

Daniel   Uh-uh.

Richard   Penny?

Daniel   No, the other one.

Richard   You mean, Alice?

Daniel   Yes. That stupid girl. Bring her along.

Richard	You want me to bring Alice with me?
Daniel	Yes.
Richard	Snood, Alice?
Daniel	Bring her along, too. *(Pause. Richard realizes.)*
Richard	Snood!
Daniel	*Just bring her along, okay?!*
Richard	Okay. Okay.
Daniel	Thanks, Richard.
Richard	Goodnight, Snood.
Daniel	Yeah, Richard. Sleep well.
Richard	You, too. *(Richard exits. Daniel watches after him...)*

Scene 2
1 Girl and 1 Boy
Daniel and Alice (both age 12)

Just before this next scene, Daniel has been seen flying in public for the first time, and now all the other children are aware of his special abilities. Afterwards, Alice returns home by herself, feeling a little lonely, and thinking alot about Daniel. Much to her surprise, when she enters her room she finds Daniel there waiting for her in the darkness! He has flown all the way from Hatch's cliff through her bedroom window, just so he can ask her a very special question.

(...Alice enters bedroom. Stands in darkness. Goes to close window.)

Daniel	Don't close it, Alice. I won't be able to get out. *(Alice cries out.)*
Alice	Who's there?

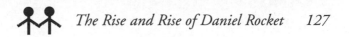

Daniel	It's me, Alice.
Alice	How did you get in?
Daniel	How do you think?
Alice	I don't know.
Daniel	Oh, Alice. You do. I flew straight through your window, into your bedroom. As if it was something I've always dreamed of. *(Pause)* Which, of course, it is, Alice. You know that.
Alice	Yes. I do. *(Pause)*
Daniel	I won't accept less than what I want, Alice.
Alice	That's good, Daniel.
Daniel	I've decided that.
Alice	That's good if it's good for you. *(Pause)* They were looking all over for you. The boys.
Daniel	Yes.
Alice	They've given up now, I think.
Daniel	Then I can go home.
Alice	You can.
Daniel	Yes.
Alice	But I'd stop off at Richard's and tell him you're alright. He was very worried about you.
Daniel	Was he?
Alice	Yes.
Daniel	Poor Richard. He worries about me alot. Too

	much, I think. Because I…I can pretty well take care of myself, Alice.
Alice	I know that.
Daniel	I think you're beginning to. *(Pause)*
Alice	So, you can fly.
Daniel	Yes.
Alice	You can actually fly.
Daniel	Mmn.
Alice	You built wings and with them you've flown. *(Pause)* Where…where are your wings, Daniel?
Daniel	I left them down by the rushes.
Alice	The rushes?
Daniel	Yes.
Alice	But, then—how…
Daniel	A secret, Alice. There's something else nobody knows. And I'm going to tell *you*. *(Pause)* The truth is, I can fly without the wings, Alice. I can fly all by myself. It's something I've…always been able to do… *(Pause)*
Alice	I thought so.
Daniel	Yes.
Alice	I just thought so.
Daniel	Mmn.
Alice	I remember that time I walked in on you, standing on top of Mrs. Rice's desk…

Daniel	Waving my arms.
Alice	Waving your arms.
Daniel	Up and down.
Alice	Up and down, yes. I saw this look, in your eyes, when you turned towards me. It was then, I guess, that I knew. *(Pause)* When did you first realize…
Daniel	A long time ago.
Alice	When you were very little?
Daniel	First grade, Alice.
Alice	First grade?!
Daniel	It's true.
Alice	You were lying in bed…
Daniel	I was in my pajamas.
Alice	And you just floated?
Daniel	Well, I felt like I wanted to fly.
Alice	You just felt like it?
Daniel	I *wanted* to. Alot.
Alice	So, you stood on the bedpost.
Daniel	And I lifted up my arms.
Alice	And then what happened?
Daniel	I flew. *(Pause)* It's been even scarier these times.
Alice	These times?
Daniel	Scarier than the first time, I mean.

Alice	The first time?
Daniel	The very first time. When we were in kindergarten. I floated once, around the sandbox. I was glad I didn't go very high. Besides, Mrs. Klinger saw me.
Alice	Mrs. Klinger?
Daniel	She had her heart attack the very next day.
Alice	You're kidding, Snood.
Daniel	No.
Alice	That's terrible.
Daniel	Yes.
Alice	And you blamed yourself.
Daniel	All these years.
Alice	That's *terrible,* Snood.
Daniel	For a long time I didn't want to fly. But I want to fly now. *(Pause)* It's just something I've had locked inside me, Alice. And now that I've let it out, there's no telling what wonderful things I can do…
Alice	Besides, with wings you can control wherever you're going.
Daniel	Yes. With wings I can go wherever I want to. *(Pause)* It's a nice night out, isn't it?
Alice	Yes.
Daniel	With the stars. And the moon. A nice time for a little flight, don't you think?
Alice	I suppose.

Daniel	Would you care to join me?
Alice	Are you serious?
Daniel	I could lift you up. On my back. I'm strong enough now. I've been practicing.
Alice	Have you?
Daniel	So I could take you with me.
Alice	Where are you going?
Daniel	I don't know. Away. Far away.
Alice	When?
Daniel	Soon. Very soon. *(Pause)*
Alice	We can't do that, Snood.
Daniel	Why not?
Alice	Because. We're only twelve years old.
Daniel	Yes.
Alice	We've got another twenty years in us at least.
Daniel	At *least* another twenty years.
Alice	Yes.
Daniel	Well, yes. I guess. That's true. *(Pause. Daniel lowers his head. Sobs. Alice is surprised. Moves to him. Touches his head.)* It's going to be horrible…being with the other kids.
Alice	Yes.
Daniel	They already hate me.
Alice	They don't hate you.

Daniel	They do! And now that they've seen me fly...I can't stay here, Alice. I've got to go, I think. Don't you? *(Pause. Alice embraces Daniel.)*
Alice	It will be alright, Daniel. Everything will be alright.
Daniel	You sure you wouldn't like a ride?
Alice	Not tonight, Snood.
Daniel	But soon?
Alice	Soon.
Daniel	Soon! Alice! Soon! We'll both be flying, Alice! You and me! We'll both live in the sky! *(Pause)* If I *do* decide to go away, Alice, I'll come back for you someday.
Alice	You will?
Daniel	Yes. Will you come with me?
Alice	I...Yes, Daniel.
Daniel	Do you promise?
Alice	I...I'll think about it.
Daniel	Good.
Alice	We...we have a whole lifetime ahead of us, Daniel.
Daniel	Yes, I guess. We do. And now, I'm going to show you what I've wanted to show you. All these years. The special secret between you and me, Alice. The secret of what I can *really* do. *(Pause. Daniel closes his eyes. Lifts up his arms. Utters low sound. Almost a hum. He floats to the ceiling. He flies around the*

room. Alice watches, spellbound. Daniel flies out bedroom window. Alice rushes after him. Looks out window. Waves. Dog heard barking, off.)

SAMMY CARDUCCI'S GUIDE TO WOMEN
BY RONALD KIDD

In the play, *Sammy Carducci's Guide to Women*, an eleven-year-old expert on women discovers that girls are people, too. Samuele Lorenzo Carducci (better known as "Sammy") is a smooth talker and a sharp dresser; he always wears a suit and red high-top sneakers when he goes to school.

In the following scene, Sammy enlists his side-kick, Gus, to help him conduct a survey of the "women" in the cafeteria at school. But before lunch time is over, Sammy is transformed from a calm, cool expert on women—into a hapless victim of love. Thus his survey is finished forever.

2 Boys
Sammy and Gus (both age 12)

Gus	My stomach hurts. I think I ate too fast.
Sammy	You're just mad because you couldn't build a fort out of frankfurter skin. Besides, the reason we ate fast was so we could start the survey.
Gus	Why couldn't we wait till later?
Sammy	Gus, the cafeteria's a perfect place for checking out a woman. You can tell a lot by the way she eats— little things most people don't notice. For instance, does she yell at her friends with her mouth full? Does she tear up her napkin to make spit wads? Does she have a milk mustache? Take Roxie Lundquist. Ever notice the way she shapes her bread into little squares to form dice?

Gus	Hey, how does she do that?
Sammy	Or Irene Klump. See anything funny about her?
Gus	Her hair?
Sammy	No, I mean the way she eats.
Gus	But she's not eating. There's no food on her plate.
Sammy	Exactly, because she already wolfed it down. Now I ask you, what kind of person finishes lunch in three minutes flat?
Gus	We did.
Sammy	I'm talking about women.
Gus	Maybe she's doing a survey on men.
Sammy	I can see we're starting at a pretty basic level. Okay, I'm going to give you some background information on women. You might want to take notes.
Gus	Huh? Oh, right. *(He opens his notebook and pulls out a pen.)* Hey, did I show you my new pen? It writes in four colors. What color do you think I should use? Maybe red. It's kind of like blood. But my brother likes green. Of course, some people think blue is nicer. But black's easier to read.
Sammy	Gus. Are you finished?
Gus	Red. Definitely red.
Sammy	Try to concentrate.
Gus	Hey, this thing is jammed. *(He fiddles with the pen, pounding it against his palm. Sammy takes it from him, clicks it, and calmly hands it back.)*

Sammy	Okay, first off, women tend to cry a lot.
Gus	*(Writing)* ...cry...a...lot. *(He shows Sammy the page.)* Is that okay?
Sammy	Yeah, fine. Most of the time, all they think about is mushy, romantic stuff. They do things like write letters to Mel Gibson and memorize the words of their favorite love song. Women are always going on diets. But they have this uncontrollable urge to bake chocolate chip cookies. It's one of the mysteries of modern science. They go around in groups, so they've got somebody to listen when they think of things to say. Which is all the time. When they're not together, they use the phone. Basically, they're weak. And they're looking for somebody strong. That's where the two of us come in. Okay, got that so far?
Gus	Right.
Sammy	*(Looking at the notebook.)* What is this?
Gus	It's a rocket ship taking off into space. See, the ship's black, the earth's green, the sky's blue, and the rocket flames are red.
Sammy	Gus.
Gus	This pen is great for rocket ships.
Sammy	Let's try a new topic, huh?
Gus	Should I still take notes?
Sammy	Yeah, but you might want to start a new page. We're going to call this "Tips for Impressing Women."
Gus	Right.

Sammy   Okay, number one. Never carry an umbrella. It's a sign of weakness.

Gus   Wow, I never knew that.

Sammy   Number two. Always use an after-shave. Even if you don't shave. Number three. Never say, "I don't know."

Gus   What if you don't know?

Sammy   Pretend you do. Number four. Talk in a low, soft voice. This is called the Voice of Love. Women go nuts over it.

Gus   What does it sound like?

Sammy   I'll do it for you later. I don't want any women bothering me right now. Number five, and this is the most important one of all. Dare to be different.

Gus   You mean wear a suit like you do?

Sammy   Gus, that wouldn't be different. That would be the same.

Gus   Then how do I know what to do?

Sammy   It's up to you. That's the whole point. Okay, let's get to the survey.

Gus   You want me to help?

Sammy   Just take notes.

Gus   On what?

Sammy   We're going to check out the women and look for things that might be important. I'll tell you, and you write it down. For instance, stuff that would drive you crazy. Like Marsha Brennamen looks fine but has a habit of picking her ear with a paper clip. Debbie Waters seems great until she laughs, then she snorts like a pig. Or that one over there. She's way too skinny. And the woman she's with. She's...

(He stares, transfixed.)

Gus	Sammy?
Sammy	...she's beautiful.
Gus	You okay?
Sammy	*(Suddenly panicked)* She's looking at us. *(Sammy grabs Gus's notebook and pen. He looks up at the ceiling, pointing at it and moving his mouth as if he's talking to Gus.)*
Gus	What are you doing?
Sammy	*(Out of the corner of his mouth.)* Just nod and smile. Pretend we're, like, student architects checking out the building.
Gus	Hey, don't chew on my pen. You might have germs.
Sammy	*(Loudly)* Yes, of course. I see.
Gus	You see what?
Sammy	She looked away. We're clear. Come on, let's go get a candy bar.
Gus	What about the survey?
Sammy	It's finished.

(The lights go down...)

THE SANCTUARY
BY ANN E. ESKRIDGE

The Sanctuary tells the story of a bright ten-year-old boy named Frederick, who goes by the nick-name of "Little Man." Little Man has no father, but a loving mom who is often overwhelmed by the responsibilities she carries alone. Together, the two live in an inner-city neighborhood, struggling to survive.

Little Man desperately wants to believe in something *good.* The other kids in the neighborhood often make fun of him and tease him about his absent father. When he finds out in a letter from his Aunt Sophie that his father died trying to save another man's life in a barroom fight, he is both proud and relieved to know that his daddy died a hero.

Little Man has recently become curious about an elderly woman, the mysterious Mrs. Lucy Johnson. Mrs. Johnson is a destitute, (presumably) homeless woman who has built a strangely beautiful, magical sanctuary out of junk. Her sanctuary is a giant collage of boxes, shopping carts, old tires and crates painted in vivid colors and unusual symbols. Upon these cast-aways hang the photos of all sorts of people that Mrs. Johnson has collected over time: famous freedom fighters, strangers, and people from Mrs. Johnson's life.

The children in the neighborhood think of Mrs. Johnson as a scary old witch who may be capable of anything! The adults just think she's *crazy.* But as Little Man gets to know Mrs. Johnson personally, he finds that the ex-school teacher is the one adult who is able to offer him the love and guidance that he needs.

Scene 1
3 Boys
Little Man, Amon and Tico (all age 10)

In the following scene, Little Man is hanging out with two other boys, Amon and Tico, on a hot, muggy summer day. When the scene begins, Little

Man has just come from the sanctuary, where he saw Mrs. Johnson perform a strange, spiritual ritual. He tries to tell Amon and Tico all about it, but Amon and Tico have other things on their minds—like ice cream and basketball—and giving Little Man a hard time.

Tico and Amon are lounging on the abandoned car. Amon is licking an ice cream while Tico is looking at a sports magazine.

Little Man is trying to explain his encounter with Lucy Johnson.

Little Man   *(Demonstrating)* …and I'm tellin' ya, she raised her hands like this, and made the sun come out.

Tico   *(Tico shoves the magazine in Amon's face.)* You see this? You see them shoes? Betcha I can out jump and run anybody on the court.

Little Man   …And she was just talkin' to herself. Well, talkin' to somebody. But I didn't see *nobody.* And then she hums like this, hummmmmmm. Some weird kinda music. More like noise. Hummin' noises and talkin' to nobody.

Amon   *(Amon brushes the magazine aside.)* Them's nothin' man. My daddy bought me a pair of shoes cost him a hundred and fifty dollars. They do everything but fly.

Little Man   …and I *heard* she had a broom and people *seen* her on *Halloween.*

(Tico takes a sip of his pop.)

Little Man   Mrs. Falls says she's a witch. And she chased *her* with a broom. And she probably wears one of them pointy hats witches wear when they go out at night.

(Amon takes a last lick of his ice cream and tosses the stick at Little Man.)

Little Man	Watch it.
Amon	Why don't you get outta here with that silly stuff. Don't you know there's some serious business goin' on here?
Tico	Yeah, serious business. *(To Amon)* Your daddy really bought you them shoes?
Amon	*(Bragging)* Sure thing. He say I gotta have the best if I'm gonna be another Michael Jordan.
Little Man	*(Impressed)* Wow, a hundred and fifty dollars.
Amon	*(Frowning)* Butt out, little squirt.
Little Man	Who you callin' a squirt? I'm as old as you and Tico. Besides, you said I could join your gang.
Amon	*(Laughs)* We only said you could join 'cause you had money on you that day. How long ago was that, Tico?
Tico	*(Looking up from magazine)* A hundred trillion, zillion years ago.

(They both laugh.)

Little Man	*(Hurt)* That was my birthday money. Momma said to share.
Amon	*(Mimics)* And momma said to share.
Little Man	*(Puffs up, angry. He jumps up from the car and fronts Amon.)* You leave my momma outta this.
Amon	*(Grabs Little Man and pulls him closer. They're face to face.)* We ain't gonna talk about your momma. But we sure gonna talk about your daddy 'cause you ain't got one. And we do. And our daddies

take us places and do things for us. And that's why the two of us are in our gang and that's why you ain't, got it?

Little Man   *(Tries to jerk away. Struggling)* I do so have a daddy. My daddy's a hero 'cause my Aunt Sophie said so in a letter. My daddy saved his friend's life. That's how come he died a hero and your daddy just paints houses ugly colors and drinks beer all day.

(Amon is a big kid, but he's also fast. Before Little Man can get off the car, Amon grabs him by the neck and forces him down on the ground. He's sitting on top of Little Man. Tico drinks his pop and watches the action.)

Tico   Fight....fight....fight...

Amon   Take it back.

Little Man   No.

Amon   *(Amon is pounding Little Man in the back with his fist.)* Take...it...back...now...or...you're...gonna be deader than the engine of that car.

Little Man   *(Holding back the tears.)* Noooooo....

Tico   *(Tico reluctantly breaks up the fight.)* I don't wanna get into trouble 'cause of you guys. Last time you two was fightin' I got on punishment. Now, kiss and make up.

(Tico makes kissing sounds. Little Man eyes Amon. Amon eyes Little Man. Little Man sticks his hand out tentatively. Amon looks at the hand and brushes it aside. But he pulls him up off the ground.)

Amon   So, butt face, what's this about your old man?

Little Man   I ain't suppose to know but...okay. See, I found this letter and it said my daddy's a hero 'cause he

was in this bar and there was a gunfight and my
daddy faced down this gunfighter to save a friend's
life. And the gunfighter shot him. And my daddy
died...like a mangy dog but his last words was, "it
wasn't nothin." That's why my daddy is a hero.

*(Little Man puffs up proudly. He looks at Tico and Amon. Amon and Tico
are impressed.)*

Tico	Man, your daddy is a hero.
Little Man	Told you so.
Amon	*(Skeptical)* This really happened?
Little Man	*(Crosses his heart, spits in his palm and holds it up to God.)* Swear.
Amon	Well, I guess you can't help it if your dad died. 'specially the way he died. What you say, Tico? Should we let him join our gang?
Tico	You got any money on you?

(Little Man shakes his head)

Tico	What we need with a poor gang member? He don't even get an allowance. Least I get an allowance.
Amon	You get change from the store, man. Stop lyin'.
Tico	I got some don't I?
Amon	So, the man don't have money. He'll just go through an initiation.
Tico	Yeah, an in...in...yeah. You know.
Amon	You got to be *brave...bold...bad...*
Amon & Tico	To be a man.

(Tico supplies the beat while the two of them go through their ritual. They give each other five. Then raise their arms and hit fists and move their pelvis back and forth.)

Little Man   So, what I got to go through?

Tico   Yeah, I don't remember us goin' through nothin'.

Amon   *(Ever patient)* Sure you do. 'member the time we took your daddy's car keys, Tico, and drove his car around the block.

Tico   Yeah, and he took off his genuine leather hand-crafted belt and tore up my behind for it. I 'member.

Amon   See, we did something tough to prove we was worthy.

Tico   I did somethin' tough and got the mess beat outta me. What you do?

Amon   My daddy grounded me. I couldn't play basketball for a whole week.

Tico   Why is it that when you do somethin' wrong the only thing that happens to you is that you can't play basketball?

Amon   *(Amon stops suddenly and Tico almost runs into him.)* Dog breath, I got to explain everything? My daddy wants me to be a famous basketball player. That's why he buys me expensive shoes, and my very own hoop. He says that by not letting me play basketball when I'm bad, it's just more time I'll have to wait until I can become a basketball star. He says it hurts him more than it hurts me.

Little Man   Seems to me it don't hurt you at all.

Amon   We ain't talkin' 'bout me, Peewee.

Little Man	Yeah…yeah…so what do I gotta do?
Amon	How 'bout swipin' food from Mr. Thompson's store?
Tico	*(Shaking his head)* Naw, Thompson'll shoot him.
Amon	Okay, what about sneakin' in the girl's locker room at the center?
Tico	Girls jumped us. They'd kill Little Man.

(Amon stops suddenly in his tracks. The boys walk on until they realize he's not with them.)

Little Man	What is it Amon? You got a idea?
Amon	*(Amon looks in the direction of Mrs. Johnson's house.)* You say you a good friend of Mrs. Johnson?
Little Man	*(Squeaks)* No.
Amon	*(Puts his arm around Little Man.)* Then this is what you gotta do. You gotta go over there and knock down that pile of junk she got and take somethin'…like a prize of war.

(Little Man tries to walk away from Amon, but Amon has a strong grip.)

Tico	Yeah, that'd be it.
Little Man	But…but…she…a…witch.
Amon	So? You ain't scared is ya?
Tico	Yeah, you ain't scared?
Amon	Besides, we'll be right behind you.
Tico	*(Startled)* We will?
Amon	Sure we will. *(He nudges Tico. Tico gets it.)*

Tico   Oh, yeah. We will.

(They push Little Man forward.)

Amon   *(Whispering)* Here's our chance. She ain't here.
                       When I count to three we start yellin' and then we
                       take it...Got it? *(Pause)* One...

Little Man   Wait a minute...wait a minute. What if she brings
                       down a lightning bolt on me and I fall down dead?

Amon   Then you'll die a man...TWO! THREE!

*(Amon pushes Little Man forward. Little Man runs, screaming a blood
curdling yell.)*

Scene 2
2 Boys
Little Man and Amon (both age 10)

In this next scene, Amon apologizes to Little Man for his remarks in the
previous scene. In doing so, Amon reveals a side of himself that he has never
shown to anyone before, and he becomes a better friend to Little Man.

At this point in the play, Mrs. Johnson has befriended Little Man and her
sanctuary has become like a second home to him. Tragically, when the
neighborhood "clean-up committee" threatens to tear down her beloved
sanctuary, Mrs. Johnson disappears from the neighborhood, leaving Little
Man devastated and alone. When this next scene opens, Little Man is
feeling abandoned.

*Little Man is sitting on the abandoned car when Amon comes up to him,
bouncing a basketball.*

Little Man   What you want?

Amon   *(Mumbles)* My dad told me to say that I was sorry
                       for saying those things about your dad.

(He waits.)

Amon	So, you comin' to the basketball game with me and Tico?
Little Man	Don't want to.
Amon	I said I was sorry.
Little Man	That ain't got nothin' to do with it.
Amon	Then what's with you?
Little Man	Nothin'.
Amon	I don't wanna go either.

(Amon sits down and bounces the ball.)

Little Man	How come?

(Amon kicks the ball away.)

Amon	*(Shrugs)* I'm sick of basketball.
Little Man	So, how come you sick of basketball?
Amon	You promise you won't tell?

(Little Man crosses his heart and spits in his hand.)

Amon	It was okay until my dad started makin' me work at it. He wants me to be a big time basketball player like he was…I suck.
Little Man	I thought you liked playing basketball. That's what you keep tellin' me and Tico.
Amon	Yeah, I know. *(Beat)* Tell you another secret?
Little Man	What?
Amon	You know all them times I get on punishment?
Little Man	Yeah.

Amon	Well, I do somethin' bad to get on punishment so I don't have to play.
Little Man	So, how come you don't tell him you don't wanna play basketball no more?
Amon	*(Hangs his head)* 'Cause I'll hurt his feelin's. He got his mind made up. He got it all figured out. How I'm gonna be a high school star and then I go to college on a scholarship and then I go pro. Never asked me if that's what I wanted.
Little Man	Life sucks.
Amon	You got that right.
Little Man	So, what you wanna do? Like, what's your purpose and all?
Amon	My what?
Little Man	Yeah, like what do you really…really…really… more than anything else…want to do?

(Amon puzzles over this.)

Amon	You know when our class went to see that play? *(Pause)* I wanna be an actor.
Little Man	*(Laughs)* You crazy, man.
Amon	*(Hurt)* What's so funny? Plenty people are actors. See it all the time on television and in the movies and in plays.

(Little Man rolls on the ground, laughing.)

Amon	You laugh some more, I'm gonna bust your jaw. It ain't funny. You asked me and I told you.
Little Man	Okay…okay…I'm sorry.

(He tries to control himself.)

Amon   What's so wrong about bein' an actor? You get to dress up in different clothes and be different people. And…and…if you're good people stand up and clap for you. *(Pause)* Bet I'd be a good actor. Watch this.

(Amon jumps up. He paces back and forth, getting into the mood. Then he strikes a majestic pose. Then flails his arms wildly.)

Amon   To be…or not to be…that is the question. Whether it is nobler in the mind to suffer the slings and arrows of outrageous and uh…something. I can't remember the rest.

Little Man   That's pretty good. What's it mean?

(Amon shrugs and sits down.)

Amon   I don't know. I asked the librarian to give me the best play ever written. She give me that. Says it's by Shakespeare. Says anybody can play Shakespeare can play anything. So, I figure to learn the hard stuff first. Then the easy stuff come easy, you know what I mean?

Little Man   Make sense to me. *(Beat)* So, how come you don't tell your dad?

Amon   You know what them actors wear in that play? They wear tights and little skirts and such. I tell my dad I gotta wear tights and a skirt he gonna put me on punishment 'til I'm collectin' social security. You be glad you don't have no dad. They make life real rough. Sometimes havin' no dad's better than havin' one.

Little Man   Life sucks.

Amon	You got that right.
(Silence)	
Little Man	Grown ups can be a real disappointment. Like finding out there ain't no Santa Claus.
Amon	Or that your favorite rap star don't even write his own stuff.
Little Man	Or that those toys you see on television don't do half the stuff they suppose to do when you take them home.
Amon	Yeah, you think you got grown ups all figured out. Next thing you know they doin' something stupid.
Little Man	*(Under his breath)* Like go crazy on you.
Amon	You say something?
Little Man	I said, if we don't go to the game, maybe we can go to see that library lady and have her give us some plays that make sense.
Amon	I got to get on punishment first.
Little Man	Okay, you get on punishment. I'll meet you there in half an hour.

(Light fades out.)

SCARS & STRIPES
BY THOMAS CADWALEDER JONES

A black urban girl and a white rural boy meet by accident in front of the Vietnam Veteran's Memorial in Washington, D.C., where they search for clues to their fathers' pasts. What begins as a hostile encounter fraught with racism and mistrust eventually develops into a strong friendship which is based on mutual respect, understanding and compassion.

In the following excerpt, the boy, *P.T.*, and the girl, *Jewel,* have spent several hours together. It is at this point in the play that their defenses have begun to melt and they are able to understand one another.

1 Boy and 1 Girl
P.T. and Jewel (young teens)

Location: The Vietnam Veteran's Memorial.

The boy is reading names on the Memorial. He has been there for a awhile. The girl watches him.

Girl	There's a directory.
Boy	I know that.
Girl	All you have to do is look up his name. It'll tell you where it's located.
Boy	Didn't you hear me, I know that—
Girl	Then, do it.
Boy	Told you this was special.
Girl	So?
Boy	So what's special about looking up his name in

	some directory and walking right up to it? No, I'm gonna start at one end an' read every one of those names till I find his.
Girl	That could take you a rather long time.
Boy	I got time.

(Silence. He moves closer to the wall, and begins to read the names. He mouths them silently to himself. She watches, finally speaks. She's been thinking this for some time now.)

Girl	Mr. P.T. Flagg from Arkansas, may I ask you a personal question?

(He ignores her and continues reading the names.)

♈♈♈♈

Girl	When exactly did your father die?
Boy	Don't know.
Girl	Your grandpa didn't tell you?
Boy	Nobody ever told me anything.
Girl	Weren't there letters? Didn't you father ever write?
Boy	If he did, grandpa sorta censored the mail.
Girl	Why would he do that?
Boy	Because he hated my dad for runnin' off to that war and he hated me for lookin' like him.
Girl	What about that other boy?
Boy	What other boy?
Girl	Your dad's friend. Didn't you ever ask him about your dad?

Boy	They went over there together.
Girl	Oh.
Boy	I guess 'cause they were buddies, best friends, something like that. When Topper finally came back home, I was really little. But I sure remember what he looked like when they took him off that bus. I was standing there, staring, thinking how he sure didn't look like Marlon Brando anymore. How he sure couldn't ride that motorcycle of his ever again. People round town said his family just sorta parked his wheelchair in an upstairs corner room, and that's where he stayed till he died.
Girl	They abandoned him?
Boy	Something like that. I remember seeing something standing under a hickory tree, in the Williams' front yard, for years after that. It was all covered up with an old, green piece've canvas. One spring we had this big storm, and it blew the green canvas off. There was this bright shiny black Harley-Davidson motorcycle standing there.
Girl	The one in the picture.
Boy	Funny thing was, nobody ever put the tarp back on it after that. Boy, I wanted that motorcycle bad. Another spring we had a big storm, and it blew the motorcycle over. One school morning, there it was, lying on its side. I kept wondering when somebody was gonna come out of that house and set that motorcycle back up, but nobody ever did. So one morning I went by there and jumped the fence and wrestled that motorcycle back up on its tires.
Girl	Good for you.

Boy   You like that, huh?

Girl   Well, somebody should've done something.

Boy   After Topper died, they put a sign on that motor-
                 cycle. Hand lettered. Black paint on a white board.
                 "For Sale—Cheap." C.H.E.—E. P. Even I knew
                 that's spelled wrong.

Girl   You should've bought it.

Boy   I did.

Girl   Good for you again.

Boy   Well, I had that picture of my dad and him and
                 they're friends. I just bought it to keep somebody
                 else from buying it. It wasn't worth anything, tires
                 all rotted out...

Girl   But you bought it; that's what counts.

Boy   I musta pushed that motorcycle 'bout seven miles
                 out of town. Took forever 'cause of those flat tires.
                 Draped a worn-out American flag over it, I'd took
                 off the pole at the high school. Made up a little
                 prayer. Pushed it off an overhang out by the highway
                 40 bridge into the East Fork of the White River.

Girl   It was a good thing you did.

Boy   When I was little, I knew about the war. I asked
                 grandpa if they were gonna send me over there like
                 my dad. He just laughed. "Not till you're eighteen,
                 boy." He said. "...Not till you're eighteen..."

Girl   I asked my mother that, when I was little, if they
                 sent girls to fight in wars.

Boy   What'd she tell you?

Girl	"Not if you're good and you eat your spinach." *(Laughs)* She was always saying things like that when I was little. Things that didn't make a lot of sense. She laughed alot, too. Then along came my stepfather and everything changed…

(Silence. They regard each other. He thinks she's told him something; he's not sure what. He resumes his search of the wall.)

Boy	I never dreamed 58,000 was so many names…I wish…
Girl	Careful what you wish, it might come true.
Boy	…If everybody who made the wars had to read all those names…
Girl	One by one…like you're doing…
Boy	Maybe there wouldn't be any more wars, huh? If they had to spend a minute with every name… All 58,000…thinking about the ones who died. …Bout how long you think that'd take anyway?
Girl	…Forty-two days…
Boy	Forty-two…You do that in your head?
Girl	58,000 minutes…divided by sixty is 966 hours… divided by twenty-four…that's forty-two days…If you spend a minute looking at each name, you're gonna be here a long, long time; I'll say that for you.
Boy	A while back, I thought I'd lost my place. Got to thinking maybe I'd looked right past his name, missed seeing it, didn't even recognize it, when I came to it. All these names start runnin' together, if you don't find one you know.

Girl	…Look. Come over here for a minute…I want to show you something.
Boy	I'll lose my place.
Girl	No, you won't, I know which panel you stopped on. Come on over here.
Boy	*(He goes to her)* Okay, what?
Girl	Look right up there. *(She points to a special place on the wall.)*
Boy	Where?
Girl	Right there. There's my father. Julius A. Robinson. See?
Boy	Yeah.
Girl	Now that's a name for you to know. Because you kinda know me.

(Suddenly, his face changes.)

Boy	Oh, my…
Girl	What?
Boy	Oh, my goodness…
Girl	What's wrong?
Boy	Look…Oh, my God, look….
Girl	It's two lines down…
Boy	My father's name.
Girl	Phineas T. Flagg…
Boy	It's him…

Girl   I must have seen it a hundred times before…It just never meant anything to me until now.

Boy   That's him; it's gotta be…

Girl   The boy in that picture…

Boy   Oh, God, that's him, that's my dad.

Girl   *(Staring at the wall.)* He died in sixty-nine.

Boy   Yeah.

Girl   Same year my father was missing.

Boy   I found it. I found his name…

(Lights fade on the two children staring up at the wall.)

SCIENTIST MEETS FISH
BY SUSAN KIM
(FOR CHRIS HANSEN, AGE 10)

The short play, *Scientist Meets Fish,* by Susan Kim was written for ten year-old Chris Hansen as part of The 52nd Street Project's One-on-One program. The 52nd Street Project brings New York City youngsters together with professional theater artists to create theater. The One-on-One program is designed to give each youngster the experience of success on stage. During one week stays in the country a youngster is paired with an adult theater professional who writes a one-act play for them to perform together. Each playwright writes a play specifically designed for the youngster with whom he or she is working, taking that young person's personal traits and capabilities into consideration. *Scientist Meets Fish* gave Chris a theatrical opportunity to shed his tough piranha exterior and become a true artist.

For more information about The 52nd Street Project, contact:
The 52nd Street Project
220 West 42nd Street
18th Floor
New York, NY 10036
(212) 764-1379

1 Girl and 1 "Piranha"
Eggfoot and Perry (any age)

(In darkness: generic jungle walla and the sound of a turbulent river.)

(Lights up. Dr. Stephanie Eggfoot, wearing khaki shorts, t-shirt and pith helmet, stands atop a raft. Her footing looks pretty wobbly.)

Eggfoot   Oh, great. Here I am, up the Amazon River without a paddle—again. I don't even know where I am. Some explorer. Why does this always happen to me? Hello? Anyone out there? Maybe if I swam to shore over there...*(She dips her toe in)* Eeeyew! It's so slimy!

161

(Perry enters, swimming. He is a fish: dressed in greenish grey, maybe with flippers and goggles. If he could have little fangs, that would be great.)

Perry   Well, well. If it isn't a human being.

Eggfoot   Who's that?

Perry   It's me. *(Eggfoot looks around)* Over here. In the water. *(He waves.)*

Eggfoot   Merciful heavens! It's a talking fish!

Perry   *(Swims on his back)* My name's Perry. What's yours?

Eggfoot   Stephanie Eggfoot. <u>Dr.</u> Stephanie Eggfoot.

Perry   Welcome to the Amazon, Dr. Eggfoot. Boy, we haven't had a doctor in years. *(To himself)* And he was pretty bland.

Eggfoot   What was that?

Perry   I said, isn't the weather *grand?*

Eggfoot   I suppose. You see, I'm called Dr. Eggfoot, but I'm not a *real* doctor. Not like you go to when you're sick. I just happen to have a degree in bio-eco-lepidopterology.

Perry   Sounds cool.

Eggfoot   *(Falsely modest)* Oh, it's nothing fancy. And you, Perry? What do you do for a living?

Perry   Who, me? I'm just a piranha.

Eggfoot   What was that?

Perry   *(Louder)* I said, I just *love* bananas!

Eggfoot   Well, they're all right, I suppose, although I prefer plantains…

Perry	So. You look like you're about to go for a swim.
Eggfoot	I was thinking of it.
Perry	Don't let me stop you.
Eggfoot	Well—I'm lost, you see; and I thought the first stop would be to get to that shore over there. How's the water?
Perry	It's great.
Eggfoot	Not too chilly?
Perry	Not to me. But I'm a fish.
Eggfoot	Yes. That's true. Well, in that case, here goes. One for the money, two for the show, three to get ready, and four to… *(She gets ready to dive. He watches her intently, smacking his lips.)* Is something wrong?
Perry	No.
Eggfoot	Then what are you staring at?
Perry	Nothing. Was I staring?
Eggfoot	What are you hanging around waiting for?
Perry	Dinner.
Eggfoot	Oh. I see. *(Gets ready to dive and stops.)* I'm sorry. What kind of fish did you say you were again?
Perry	…a goldfish.
Eggfoot	A goldfish? Then how come you're *green*?
Perry	…I rusted?
Eggfoot	Gold doesn't rust.

Perry	…I'm seasick?
Eggfoot	That sounds highly unlikely…
Perry	I'm really jealous?
Eggfoot	Wait a minute… "you just love bananas"… I get it! Banana my foot! You're a *piranha!* And you want to eat me for dinner!
Perry	Kind of. You don't mind, do you?
Eggfoot	Mind? Of course I mind! My parents didn't raise me to be fish food for some…flounder!
Perry	Look. I'm not crazy about the idea either—but I'm starving! I haven't eaten in days!
Eggfoot	Oh, thank you. I feel so much better knowing it's not personal.
Perry	I can't help being a cold-blooded killer. You know what they say about the rainforest…
Eggfoot	Don't say it!
Eggfoot & Perry	"It's a jungle out here."
Eggfoot	I *knew* you were going to say that!
Perry	Besides, I'm not really a killer. I'm just food patrol.
Eggfoot	What's that mean?
Perry	I swim around until I find food for the rest of the guys. Only I keep messing up.
Eggfoot	What do you do wrong?
Perry	I let everything escape. Monkeys. Parrots. A guy from National Geographic.

Eggfoot	Why do you do that?
Perry	I dunno. I guess I felt bad for them.
Eggfoot	But you're a piranha. Piranhas are professional killing machines.
Perry	Some killing machine. You want to know a secret?
Eggfoot	What?
Perry	I'm a vegetarian. But don't tell anyone.
Eggfoot	Are you serious? Well, in that case…if you really are hungry…would you like some of my peanut butter sandwich?
Perry	Peanut butter sandwich? Who's he?
Eggfoot	It's not a he. Here. *(She takes out a "sandwich" and gives him half. He "eats.")*
Perry	Hey—this is pretty good!
Eggfoot	You know what I think? I don't think you're a cold-blooded killer. Sure you're a piranha. But you're something *more* than just a scary fish with big teeth. Aren't you?
Perry	Well. Can I tell you another secret?
Eggfoot	Sure.
Perry	I never wanted to be a piranha.
Eggfoot	What did you want to be?
Perry	Don't laugh. *(Eggfoot shakes her head "no.")* I always wanted to be…a painter.
Eggfoot	Really?

Perry	Yeah. But it's tough when you live in a river. All that water, it's a real mess…
Eggfoot	You could always use a pencil.
Perry	I do. You wanna see some of my pictures? I hide them 'cause the guys always make fun of me. *(He swims to the wings and retrieves some big "pictures.")*
Eggfoot	Hey—these are really good. *(She examines picture of a fish.)* I like this one. Who's this?
Perry	That's my brother.
Eggfoot	*(Examining a picture of another fish.)* And who's this?
Perry	That's my other brother.
Eggfoot	Do they all really have three little hairs growing out of their heads?
Perry	Naw. I just added those.
Eggfoot	Hey, Perry—I think you should be an artist full-time.
Perry	Nawww.
Eggfoot	I'm serious. These are great. You could come with me.
Perry	Really? And people wouldn't laugh?
Eggfoot	No, are you kidding? A painting piranha? You could probably get federal funding and everything.
Perry	Well…
Eggfoot	Only problem is…I don't know how to get out of here. I dropped my map when my paddle fell in the water. I'm totally lost.

Perry	Well…would this be any help? *(He holds out a map.)*
Eggfoot	Good golly, Perry! It's a map! Where'd you get this?
Perry	I drew it.
Eggfoot	Wow! And it's accurate and everything?
Perry	Yep. It's to "scale."
Eggfoot	Well, in that case…how should we do this?
Perry	Can you swim?
Eggfoot	Sure! Only…is it safe?
Perry	With me around? No sweat! *(He holds out his arm for her to take.)* I'll be your escort.
Eggfoot	Well, okay. Here goes, I guess… *(She kicks off her shoes.)*
Perry	And Stephanie?
Eggfoot	Yes?
Perry	You're really serious about people not laughing?
Eggfoot	I'm totally serious. *(Starts to dive, then stops.)* And Perry?
Perry	Yes?
Eggfoot	You're really serious about being a vegetarian?
Perry	You bet. But maybe you should bring the rest of the sandwich—okay?
Eggfoot	Okay! *(She jumps in.)* Wow! It's nice and cool! Which way to Miami?
Perry	This way! To Miami!

Eggfoot   To art!

Perry   To art!

Eggfoot   Hey—wait up!

(They exit, swimming. Blackout.)

THE SECRET GARDEN
SCREENPLAY
BY CAROLINE THOMPSON
BASED ON THE BOOK
BY FRANCES HODGSON BURNETT

Originally a novel, *The Secret Garden* tells the much-loved story of Mary, a young girl living in England at the turn of the century. Although Mary is English, most of her childhood was spent in India, where she lived with her wealthy, socialite parents and her Indian servant, Ayah. This was during a period of history in which England occupied and ruled India.

While in India, however, Mary's family and village is unexpectedly stricken with a plague—and dies. Mary is the sole survivor of the plague, and, having nowhere else to go, is shipped back to England, to live with her uncle on his large estate in the country.

When she arrives there, however, she finds that it is not the comfortable, welcoming home that she had hoped so much for. The weather is cold and gray, all the shrubbery is wilted, and the halls of the mansion are dark and gloomy. She is locked in her room for hours at a time by the hard-hearted housekeeper, Mrs. Medlock. But worst of all, late at night, when she is lying in her bed, she can hear the ghostly sound of crying...and no one will tell her who or what it is.

Gradually Mary's life begins to change for the better. She makes friends with a young boy named Dickon, who helps her to find the doorway into a magical, secret garden. In the garden, life is joyous, and the bleakness of the cold winter gives way to hope and the coming spring.

Just before the following excerpt begins, Mary once more awakens to the haunting sound of crying. Disturbed and curious, she sneaks out of bed and follows the noise, determined to find its source. Mary walks through a series of dark and dusty hallways, past spider webs and creaking doors...and when she finally does find what she is looking for, Mary is amazed indeed.

4 Scenes for
1 Girl and 1 Boy
Mary and Colin

Mary, holding a lantern, makes her way towards a room. The sound of crying is very near now. Mary sees light coming from beneath a door, part way down the hallway. The crying is coming from that room. The voice is clearly a child's.

A low fire glows in the hearth illuminating an immense room with ancient handsome furniture in it. There is a bed at the far end. The crying comes from there. As much as Mary has been seeking its source, finding it still startles her—and she gasps.

Hearing her, the occupant of the bed—a boy—also gasps. The crying catches in his throat. He freezes.

Colin   *(In a frightened whisper.)* Are you a ghost?

Mary   *(In her own frightened whisper.)* No. Are you?

Colin   Who are you? What are you doing here?

Mary	I live here. Who are *you*?
Colin	I am master of this house while my father's away.
Mary	Your *father*? He's my uncle! Nobody told me he had a son.

(A beat)

Colin	Come here. *(Mary crosses the room part way.)* What's your name?
Mary	I'm Mary Lenox.
Colin	I've never heard of you.
Mary	What's your name?
Colin	Colin Craven. I still can't see you.

(Mary moves closer to the bed. Just as the boy can now see her, so she can now see him. He has a sharp, delicate, very pale face and his gray eyes open so wide they look immense.)

Mary	I've never heard of you either.
Colin	But you're my cousin…
Mary	Our mothers were sisters. Twins.
Colin	Twins? Nobody told me she had a twin.
Mary	Why were you crying?
Colin	I can't sleep. Plump my pillows for me, Cousin Mary.
Mary	What?
Colin	My pillows… And the covers have gotten all twisted.
Mary	Well, I don't know what to do about it. I'll get Martha or Mrs. Medlock.

Colin	No!
Mary	Why not?
Colin	Medlock wouldn't allow you in here. She'd be afraid you'd upset me and make me even *more* ill.
Mary	Do I? I'll go.
Colin	Stop! Stay here. How old are you?
Mary	Ten.
Colin	We're the same age. *(He stares and stares at her.)* What's your mother like?
Mary	She's dead.
Colin	Mine's dead too.

(He points to a cord on a silk curtain that hangs over the mantelpiece.)

Colin	See that cord?

(Mary looks)

Colin	Pull it.

(Mary crosses to the cord. She pulls it... The silk curtain runs back on rings, uncovering a painting of Colin's mother.)

Colin	That's my mother. Did your mother look like her?

(Mary nods. She can't take her eyes off the painting.)

Mary	Why do you keep a curtain over her?
Colin	She smiles too much.
Mary	Smiles too much? How can anybody smile too much?
Colin	Sometimes I hate her. She died when I was born.

Mary	*(It slips out.)* But I thought she died in her garden…
Colin	Her garden? What garden?
Mary	*(Covering her mistake.)* Oh…just a garden. There are so many of them here.
Colin	Are there?
Mary	Of course. Don't you ever go outside?
Colin	Never!
Mary	Why not? What's the matter with you?
Colin	I'm going to die.
Mary	From what?
Colin	From everything. I've spent my whole life in this bed.

(Mary sees the wheelchair in a corner of the room.)

Mary	You don't know how to walk?

(Colin shakes his head.)

Colin	*(Urgently)* You *are* real aren't you? My dreams are so real sometimes…
Mary	Shall I pinch you to prove it? *(Pinches him.)*
Colin	Ow!
Mary	See?

(Mary giggles. Even Colin looks on the verge of smiling—he's never met anyone like this girl.)

Colin	Will you come visit me? Will you come every day? …Though I don't know what Medlock would do if she found out…

Mary	We won't tell her.
Colin	Or anybody else.
Mary	It'll be another secret.
Colin	Another?

(Mary stammers—thinking of the garden, but not wanting to mention it again.)

Mary	Your portrait's a kind of secret. You were a secret from me and I was a secret from you…
Colin	But not anymore. We're the ones with the secrets now.

(Mary bites her lip…yes, indeed……)

�psℝ♀♀♀

In the following scene, Mary tries to get Colin to stop taking himself so seriously.

(Dark wooden shutters cover the windows in Colin's bedroom. Mary hurries into view, grabbing ahold of them.)

Mary	At least we can open the windows. Just wait until you see. Dickon says—

(She goes to open them)

Colin	No! Get away from there! Don't touch them! They're nailed shut! My lungs! They can't take the spores!
Mary	Spores?
Colin	They're carried in on the wind, and when you breathe the air, you swallow them. They stick in your lungs.
Mary	But before I got out into the wind even my hair was scrawny.

Colin	Your hair? Hair is dead.
Mary	If hair is dead, how comes it keeps on growing, even after you die? *(Laughs)* Well…maybe not *your* hair. By then you might be bald.
Colin	Don't be stupid. I'll be dead before I'm old enough to be bald. I'll get a hump on my back like my father and then I'll die…
Mary	I hate the way you talk about dying…
Colin	Everybody thinks I'll die—
Mary	*(As contrary as ever.)* If everybody thought that about me, I wouldn't do it.

(He pulls a face mask out of his drawer.)

Colin	Put this on. Everybody has to wear one. Medlock's orders.
Mary	But she's not here to see me.
Colin	Put it on!

(She takes it from him and grimaces as she ties it on.)

Mary	It makes my face itch! *(She instantly tears it off.)* I can't stand it! I didn't give you any germs last night, did I?
Colin	Put on the mask!
Mary	Stop talking to me as if you were a Rajah with emeralds and diamond and rubies stuck all over you!
Colin	I'll talk to you any way I please.

(Indignant, she marches toward the door.)

Colin	Where are you going?
Mary	Back outside to be with Dickon.
Colin	*(Makes a face.)* Dick-on…
Mary	*(Defensive)* He tames animals like the animal charmers in India. And he knows everything there is to know about gardens—
Colin	*(Interrupts)* Does he know about my mother's garden?
Mary	What?
Colin	You told me my mother had a garden.
Mary	*(Trying to cover this information.)* How would he know about it? It's locked. No one's allowed in there.
Colin	Well *I* can make them unlock it.
Mary	No, don't! Don't do that!
Colin	Why not?
Mary	If you make them open the door like that, if every one knows, it wouldn't be a secret any more. Don't you see how much better it is if it's a secret?

(Colin hesitates.)

Mary	You *have* to! Maybe you can't even keep a secret!

🌳🌳🌳🌳

In this next scene, Mary visits Colin in his room on a rainy night.

(It's dark in the room but for the glow of firelight and quiet but for the pelting of rain outside. Mary listens at the shuttered window.)

Mary	In India when it rained, my Ayah would tell me

stories. *(She goes to Colin's bed and climbs up onto it with him.)*

Colin   About what?

Mary   The gods and goddesses mostly…In one of the stories, there was even a God who sort of reminds me of you.

Colin   Really? How?

Mary   When he was growing up, he had to be kept a secret, so nobody would see him or know where he was…

Colin   Why?

Mary   Because his uncle wanted to kill him. The uncle had a dream that the young God would take over Heaven.

Colin   Did the dream come true?

Mary   *(Nods)* When he was older.

Colin   Where did he hide?

Mary   He lived with some cows.

Colin   What was he like? Was he different from other people?

Mary   Only on the inside. When you looked down his throat, you could see the whole universe there.

Colin   The whole universe couldn't fit down anybody's throat.

Mary   Down *his* it could.

Colin   How? That would mean he'd have to be bigger than the whole universe to fit the universe down his throat and you said he looked like everybody else on the outside.

Mary   That's right. It's *inside* that he was different.

Colin   But it doesn't make sense.

Mary   It doesn't *have* to make sense, it's the idea of it.

Colin   Oh, that's stupid.

Mary   No, it's not. It's magic.

Colin   You can't really be that stupid.

Mary   I am *not* stupid! You just don't understand! You don't want to! *(She gets off the bed and heads for the door.)*

Colin   You can't leave. You wouldn't dare.

Mary   Oh, wouldn't I?

Colin   I'll have them drag you back in…

Mary   Will you, Mister Rajah? Fine! That's just fine! *(She sits stubbornly.)* Then I won't even look at you. I'll stare at the floor! I'll clench my teeth together and never tell you one thing! Not even about seeing your father!

Colin   Yes, you will. Tell me!

(Mary purses her lips and says nothing. Colin stares woefully at her.)

Colin   He didn't come to see me. He doesn't like me. I'll die because he doesn't like me.

Mary   Well, he likes me.

Colin   But he's *my* father!

Mary	Maybe if you weren't always so rude…
Colin	I'm not rude.
Mary	Yes you are. You're so sour, you won't even open your windows and let the sun shine into your room!
Colin	How can I? It's raining out.
Mary	Even if it weren't raining.
Colin	If it weren't raining, maybe I would.
Mary	You never have.
Colin	So why does that mean I never would?…. I am *not* sour. *(He frowns sourly.)*

In this last scene between Colin and Mary, Colin has been wailing non-stop and is still wailing when Mary storms in.

Mary	Stop it! You stop! I hate you! Everybody hates you!

(Whipping around at the sound of her voice, Colin chokes on the next scream.)

Mary	You're so selfish! You're the most selfish boy there ever was!

(Mary shouts at Colin and Colin shouts right back.)

Colin	I'm not as selfish as you are! Just because I'm always ill!
Mary	Nobody ill could scream like that!
Colin	I'm going to die!
Mary	What do you know about dying?

Colin	My *mother* died!
Mary	*Both* my parents died!
Colin	I felt a lump on my back! I'll get a hump like my father and…

(Mary prods Colin's back.)

Mary	Where?

(Mary climbs up onto the bed to pull Colin's shirt up.)

Mary	There's nothing but your bones sticking out! It's because you're so skinny.
Colin	*(With wonder)* It is?… I'm not ill?
Mary	I don't see how. You're just weak.
Colin	Do you think maybe I could go outside? Spores and all?
Mary	*(Giggles with relief.)* I don't know anything about spores.
Colin	If I went out, we could find the door to my mother's garden. *(Mary bites her lip.)* If we found the door, we could go inside…

(Mary looks away—avoiding his gaze.)

Colin	What is it?
Mary	I didn't dare tell you. I didn't, 'cause I was so afraid I couldn't trust you—for sure.
Colin	What?
Mary	I've been in the secret garden. I found the key. Weeks ago…

(But Colin is excited rather than angry.)

Colin   Tell me! Go on…

Mary   When you open the door, you can't see anything.
                  Then you walk down a long staircase. At the bottom,
                  you realize that you're right in the middle of the
                  ruins of an old church. Did you know there used
                  to be a church here?

(Colin shakes his head no.)

Mary   It must have been in ruins for a long time. Most
                  of it has fallen down. Plants and grass are growing
                  everywhere, all over it… Dickon was right. He
                  said spring would start over again after the rains—
                  and it has. Every day new flowers open. It's like
                  magic. Baby animals are being born.

Colin   I'll go out there! I'll go in my chair! Perhaps I'll go
                  every day!

THE SNOWFLAKE
AVALANCHE
BY Y YORK

Ten-year-old Tim, an only child, lives with his parents in a Long Island suburb. Tim's father, an attorney, is involved in the legal defense of Thomas, a Native American man charged with murder. Thomas killed the President of an oil company after a devastating oil spill permanently destroyed the coastal environment of his small Pacific Northwestern fishing town. Now imprisoned on the charge of murder, Thomas awaits trial. His wife, Janet, and their baby, come to New York for the trial, and, having nowhere else to go, stay in Long Island with Tim's family.

During that time, Janet gets Tim involved in a plan to stop the contamination of the water in the area. In doing so, she teaches Tim a new way of looking at life and at the planet.

In the following scene, Janet teaches Tim a Native American ritual, the "Give-Away Ceremony."

Special Notes

The character of Janet is an adult, but this is a wonderful scene for two children to work on in a classroom situation.

1 Boy and 1 Woman
Timmy (age 10) and Janet (older)

Scene. The house. Tim with bird mask and Janet.

Tim   They'd have a party?, a party to give their stuff away?

Janet   To show off.

Tim   I don't get it. Okay, okay. So a chief, a big chief puts his stuff in a pile, invites a lot of people over, and they take it away. Is that it?

Janet   I think so.

Tim   *(Beat)* You *think?* Don't you know?

Janet   No.

Tim   You said you were an Indian.

Janet   Other tribes do it; not my one.

Tim   You never did it?

Janet   Not like this.

Tim   I think it's really stupid; giving your stuff away to show off. That's not how you show-off. That's how you show you're stupid. *You* think it's stupid, don't you?

Janet   *Showing off* is stupid.

Tim	*No, giving your stuff away* is stupid.
Janet	Let's do it.
Tim	*(Horrified)* You want me to give my stuff away?!
Janet	I'll give my stuff away.
Tim	You don't have any stuff.
Janet	I have a little bit of stuff.

(Janet takes a pen from her pocket and removes some jewelry, makes a pile.)

Janet	*(Gestures)* Welcome People. Welcome to my potlatch. I spread before you my jewels and my pen. Take what pleases you; scatter the rest to the wind.
Tim	Am I the People?
Janet	You be the People.
Tim	*(Looks at the stuff, big voice)* I take this necklace, and I take this bracelet; the pen I scatter to the winds.
Janet	I think you should take all my stuff or it's like an insult.
Tim	Okay, okay. *(Big voice)* I take the pen, too.
Janet	And I am pleased to give it to you. Next year I hope you will come and clean me out again. *(Pause)* What do you think?
Tim	*(Pause)* I think it's really stupid. I got all your stuff, and I don't even like the pen.
Janet	*(Surprised)* I kindda liked it.
Tim	I got all your stuff!

Janet	But I feel okay about it.
Tim	*(Pause, figuring it out)* Because you got to be...generous.
Janet	Yeah! That's it! They got to be generous.

SUZIE AND HER SISTERS AND THE SOCKS THAT STUCK
BY JEFF WOOD

Three sisters, an enchanted pair of socks, and a dog named "Bop" come together in more ways than one in this magical short play about the nature of love.

5 Children
Suzie, Tillie, Elsie, Narrator
and 1 "Dog" (to be played by a human being)

(A room with a couch and a coffee table. Bop the dog—who should be played by a human—is snoozing loudly on the floor, maybe chasing rabbits, having dog dreams. Suzie enters. She is wearing a pair of bright red and orange and yellow socks. During the narration she pantomimes making a bowl of cereal, then sits down to eat it.)

Narrator So there was this girl, and her name was Suzie, and she had a favorite pair of socks she wore to bed every night, because her feet got cold, and the socks were very warm. They were made of wool, and brightly colored; red at the top, orange at the heel and the toe, and yellow everywhere else. When she looked at them on her feet the colors reminded her of campfires, of kitchen stoves, of the sun when it's rising. Warm things. She loved those socks. One morning she and her socks woke up and walked into the kitchen to eat some cereal. When she was done eating she started to take off the socks, so she could put on some slippers.

(The action onstage freezes.)

Narrator   And that's when the first weird thing happened. She couldn't get them off.

(The action onstage unfreezes.)

Suzie   I can't get these off!

Narrator   It wasn't like they were glued on or anything. The wool would move easily on her skin, and she could slip her hand inside, between the sock and her foot. They just wouldn't come off. She called for her sisters, Elsie and Tillie.

Suzie   Come here Elsie! Come here Tillie! My socks are stuck!

(Elsie and Tillie enter.)

Elsie   That's goofy. Socks don't get stuck.

Suzie   These socks did.

Narrator   Elsie was Suzie's younger sister. She thought everything was goofy. Younger sisters are like that.

Tillie   You probably got jelly on your feet.

Suzie   There's no jelly on my feet. I haven't had any jelly yet. They're just stuck.

Narrator   Tillie was Suzie's older sister. She thought she knew everything. Older sisters are like that.

Tillie   They couldn't have just stuck. Socks don't do that. Socks aren't sticky. Maybe you left some candy bars in your socks.

Suzie   I don't keep candy bars in my socks.

Elsie	Maybe there's boogers in there. *(Elsie laughs. Suzie starts to cry.)*
Tillie	See what you did. You made Suzie cry.
Suzie	No one believes me.
Elsie	We believe you.
Suzie	Then help me get these off.
Tillie	Yeah. Elsie, let's help our sister.

(Elsie and Tillie each grab hold of a sock.)

Narrator	So Suzie and Elsie kneeled on the floor and they each grabbed one of this girl's socks. Then they pulled. Nothing happened. They pulled harder. Still nothing. They got to their feet and they braced themselves. They pulled and pulled. They pulled as hard as they knew how. They pulled as they never had before. But the socks stayed stuck.
Suzie	*(Sniffling)* What are we gonna do now?
Tillie	We'll think of something.
Elsie	We will?
Narrator	Elsie and Tillie started to let go of the socks.

(The action onstage freezes.)

Narrator	And that's when the second weird thing happened. Elsie and Tillie's hands were stuck to the socks.

(The action onstage unfreezes.)

Tillie	Oh, no! I'm stuck to the sock that's stuck to my sister!
Elsie	Me, too! I'm stuck to the second sock!

Suzie	I've got two socks stuck on my feet, and a sister stuck to each sock! What do we do now? This has never happened before.
Elsie	I got a waffle stuck to my stomach once.
Tillie	That's because you spilled syrup on your stomach and then dropped your waffle where the syrup was. It's not the same thing. Syrup's supposed to be sticky. But socks aren't supposed to be sticky. And sisters aren't supposed to be sticky either. There's got to be a logical explanation for all of this. Let's try an experiment.
Elsie	That's goofy. You're always so logical.
Tillie	What's wrong with being logical? Logic is good.
Elsie	Logic is worthless. The problem with logic is that it doesn't make any sense.
Tillie	You don't make any sense.
Elsie	You're retarded.
Tillie	You're smelly.
Elsie	You're ugly.
Suzie	Stop it, both of you! I think Tillie's right. What's the experiment, Tillie?
Tillie	Well, I think you should hold all sorts of different stuff, and find out what sticks, and what doesn't. You held the cereal box this morning and it didn't stick to you. Right?
Suzie	Right.
Tillie	And the bowl didn't stick to you either. Right?

Suzie	Right.
Tillie	So not everything sticks. Let's find out what sticks and what doesn't. Pick up that candle.

(Suzie picks up a candle on the coffee table.)

Tillie	Now let go.

(Suzie lets go. The candle drops.)

Tillie	Okay, candles don't stick. Try picking up the phone.

(Suzie picks up the phone.)

Tillie	Now let go.

(Suzie lets go. The phone drops.)

Tillie	Phones don't stick either. I think we can conclude scientifically from these experiments that nothing else is sticking to you.
Elsie	Thank you, Dr. Science.
Narrator	Just then their dog, who's name was Bop, woke up and walked over to see what was going on. Bop was big and old and shaggy. Bop was a pretty cool dog.

(Bop walks over to the girls.)

Suzie	Over here, Bop.
Bop	Woof.
Narrator	Suzie liked Bop a lot. Bop came over and this girl put her arms around him. It made her feel better to hug this dog she had grown up with, had spent her entire life with. Bop licked her face, and she laughed, and then tried to push his face away.

(The action onstage freezes.)

Narrator   And that's when the third weird thing happened. Suzie was stuck to Bop.

(The action onstage unfreezes.)

Suzie   Tillie! We're all stuck together! I thought you said I wasn't going to stick to anything else!

Tillie   I guess I was wrong.

Elsie   I guess you were.

Tillie   I don't understand. We can't be wrong. We used science.

Elsie   Science is for geeks.

Tillie   Let's be logical. We need to figure out why the stuff that sticks to you sticks to you. And why the stuff that doesn't stick doesn't stick.

Elsie   Logic won't work. I know why!

Tillie   What does the stuff that sticks have in common? Socks. Sisters. The dog.

Elsie   We don't need logic. I know why!

Tillie   Because they're all alive?

Elsie   That's goofy. Socks aren't alive. I know why!

Tillie   Because they all have hair?

Elsie   No, no, no. Wrong. I know why!

Tillie   *(Turning to Elsie.)* Okay. You're so smart. Tell us why. Tell us why the socks stick. Tell us why Bop sticks. Tell us why we stick.

Elsie   Because she loves us all!

Tillie   What?

Elsie   She loves us!

(The action onstage freezes)

Narrator   And that's when the last weird thing happened. Everything quit sticking.

(The action onstage unfreezes. Elsie, Tillie, and Bop all become unstuck and fly to different corners of the room. Bop starts to run around the three girls, barking.)

Elsie   That's the reason we all stuck. Because she loved us all so much she couldn't bear to let us go. She was scared of losing us.

Tillie   Is that true?

Suzie   Well, I remember feeling sad yesterday because I thought I had lost my socks. But then Mom told me to look in the laundry basket and I found them. And I was sad when you two were talking about going to camp this summer, and I was thinking how much I would miss you. And Bop, well…

Tillie   Bop's getting old.

Suzie   Bop's getting old. I guess Elsie's right. I was scared of letting you all go. I was scared of losing you.

Elsie   You won't ever lose us.

Tillie   No. Not ever. Even if we went to camp, we'd come back.

Elsie   And while we were gone we would think about you.

Tillie	And you would think about us.
Elsie	We're all stuck together, even when we're apart. Love sticks things together. It's really strong. It's so strong that the things it holds together won't ever come apart. You don't need us to stick to you. We're already stuck. Everybody's stuck to everybody else. That's life. That's what it is. We don't have any choice.
Tillie	We're stuck with each other. Even when we're not stuck *to* each other.
Suzie	Really?
Elsie	Really. We'll always be together. As together as we are in this room right now.

(Suzie takes off her socks and puts them on the floor.)

Narrator	Suzie looked around the room. Outside, the sun was climbing in the sky, and sunlight was streaming through the window. It was shining on Elsie's face, and on Tillie's face, and on Bop's face. Everyone was smiling, even Bop. They all just sat on the floor and looked at each other and smiled. In the middle of the room was the pair of wool socks, just lying there, the socks that Suzie loved so much, and she figured that if those socks had mouths they'd be smiling too.
Bop	Woof!

(Lights fade to black.)

TO BEE OR NOT TO BEE
BY SUSAN KIM
(FOR YOLANDA MOLDONADO, AGE 14)

In this short comedy, a bee disguises herself as a chipmunk in a daring attempt to survive one of the world's most famous floods—and succeeds! Like the short play *Scientist Meets Fish* (see page 161 for details), *To Bee or Not to Bee* was written as part of The 52nd Street Project's One-on-One program, this time for fourteen year-old Yolanda Moldonado.

1 Girl and 1 "Bee"
Ms. Noah and Bee (any age)

Ms. Noah, wearing a raincoat and a headset, stands by her husband's ark, holding a clipboard and pencil. She is a no-nonsense type and at the moment, looks really hassled.

Ms. Noah	Last call for all animals boarding the ark! Friends and family members NOT holding valid passes will be asked to get off the ark at this time! Passengers with valid passes, please form a single line on the ramp with your partner! Hold your passes up where I can see them, and no pushing, biting, or stampeding, please! Thank you!

She starts to check off her list.

Ms. Noah	Lizards! Kangaroos! Shetland ponies, rhinoceroses! Stop pushing, there's plenty of time! Rabbits, iguanas, bald eagles—is that your suitcase? Keep it out of the aisle, please, we got a lot of traffic coming through! Llamas! Doberman pinschers, penguins, hamsters...

(A bee, wearing a baseball cap and dark glasses, tries to walk quickly past Ms. Noah. She walks with her head lowered, and holds her pass over her head.)

Ms. Noah	Can I help you?
Bee	Chipmunk.
Ms. Noah	Excuse me?
Bee	I'm a chipmunk, my husband's on board, I just stepped off to make a few phone calls…
Ms. Noah	Wait a second. Can I see your pass?
Bee	Here. *(She flashes the pass at her.)* I'm a chipmunk. See? Here's my pass, that's my picture. Bye!
Ms. Noah	Just one second! *(She examines the pass.)* This doesn't look anything like you. What did you say you were?
Bee	I'm a chipmunk. See? *(She bares her front teeth and holds up her hands like paws.)* Whoa, there's my husband over there, gotta roll!
Ms. Noah	*(Collaring her)* Where did you say you got this?
Bee	At the main office?
Ms. Noah	You didn't get this from the main office. You made it yourself! *(Ms. Noah suddenly whips off the Bee's hat. Her antenna spring out.)* AH HAA!
Bee	Shhh!
Ms. Noah	JUST AS I THOUGHT! YOU'RE A BEE!
Bee	Not so loud!
Ms. Noah	You're a bee, and you were trying to sneak on board! Weren't you?
Bee	Hey, don't look at me! I waited for months, and I never got a form in the mail!

Ms. Noah	You never got a form because bees weren't included on the final list! See? *(Reading)* "Subsection B-1: dragons, unicorns, mermaids, and ESPECIALLY bees, NOT to be allowed on board the ark under ANY circumstances!
Bee	Oh, yeah? Well, what about him over there?
Ms. Noah	Who?
Bee	That guy over there. How come you let him on board?
Ms. Noah	He's a cockroach.
Bee	Yeah? And what about her?
Ms. Noah	She's a Tibetan beetle.
Bee	Oh, I see. So beetles and cockroaches are okay, and bees aren't?
Ms. Noah	Don't ask me. I didn't write the list.
Bee	But that doesn't make any sense! How can you let those clowns on and not someone like me? I know how to garden! I make great honey! I'm a terrific dancer!
Ms. Noah	Look. I'll tell ya. You want to know the truth, woman to bug? You make my husband nervous.
Bee	I do?
Ms. Noah	You never hang out with Noah. You never come when he whistles.
Bee	It's called being an insect. We're like that, we're very independent.

Ms. Noah	It's not just because you're a bug. Noah loves bugs, we have millions on board already. He just hates bees.
Bee	Why?
Ms. Noah	Well. If you promise not to tell. I think he was stung once. On the... *(She whispers to the bee.)*
Bee	Great. So your husband has one bad experience on a school field trip, and there goes the entire race of bees, extinct forever? Real mature.
Ms. Noah	You know, I'm starting to think I'm not too crazy about bees, either.
Bee	What's not to like?
Ms. Noah	First of all, you got too much attitude. You're pushy. Plus you complain too much. Buzz, buzz, buzz, you're giving me a headache and we're not even on board yet. Besides, it's not like you're a butterfly or a dragonfly or anything special like that. All you've got is stripes and a needle on your butt. Big deal.
Bee	But we pollinate things!
Ms. Noah	Oh, I'm really impressed. Now, do you mind? I've got an ark to fill in the next half hour, and we're only up to the penguins. Camels? Think you could step on it, please?
Bee	But you can't just throw me off! I can't swim, I don't have any water wings!
Ms. Noah	Sorry. Would you mind getting off the ark, please?
Bee	But I'll drown!

Ms. Noah	*(Into headset)* Security? Yeah, it's me. I get a disturbance on Level One F, I got a disorderly bee here who refuses to buzz off. *(She grabs the bee by the arm and starts to drag her off.)*
Bee	Help! Help, I'm an innocent chipmunk being attacked by a crazy lady! Help!
Ms. Noah	NO BEES ON BOARD AND THAT'S FINAL!
Bee	Help!

(We hear a ding.)

Voice of God	*(Amplified. She happens to be female.)* This is your deity speaking. We are currently thirty-eight minutes from the end of the world as we now know it.
Ms. Noah	God? Is that you, God?
Voice of God	For the information of all passengers, please be informed that the bee is a valuable member of my future world plans for millennia to come. As such, treat her with all due respect. And stop acting like the Queen of Sheba. *(We hear a ding.)* The Lord hath spoken.
Ms. Noah	Yes God, your honor your majesty sir. I mean ma'am. I mean…
Bee	Wow, did you hear that? So I guess I'm cool, right?
Ms. Noah	I guess. But you've got to promise me one thing.
Bee	Sure. What?
Ms. Noah	You've got to promise me that whatever happens, you and your children and your grandchildren

and your great-great-grandchildren after you must never, ever sting another human being as long as your kind exists. Not on the arm, not on the leg, and especially not on the… *(Whispers)*

Bee   I promise.

Ms. Noah   All right, then. In that case: welcome aboard.

(She exits. The bee looks at the audience and shrugs.)

Bee   So I lied.

(Blackout. End of play.)

YOU'RE A GOOD MAN, CHARLIE BROWN
BY CLARK GESNER

Based on the comic strip, "Peanuts," this musical portrays the trials and tribulations of the cartoon characters Charlie Brown, Lucy, Linus, Snoopy and others as they deal with school, baseball and friendships.

In the following scene Lucy and her younger brother Linus discuss Lucy's plans for the future.

1 Boy and 1 Girl
Linus and Lucy

Linus at home watching T.V. Lucy enters.

Lucy   Okay. Switch channels.

Linus   Are you kidding? What makes you think you can come right in here and take over?

Lucy   These five fingers, individually are nothing. But when I curl them together into a single unit they become a fighting force terrible to behold.

Linus   Which channel do you want? *(He looks at his hand.)* Why can't you guys get organized like that?

Lucy   Linus, do you know what I intend? I intend to be a queen. When I grow up, I'm going to be the biggest queen there ever was and I'll live in this big palace with a big front lawn and have lots of beautiful dresses to wear and when I go out in my coach all the people…

Linus	Lucy.
Lucy	...all the people will wave and I will shout at them, and...
Linus	Lucy, I believe "queen" is an inherited title.

(Silence)

Yes, I'm quite sure. A person can only become a queen by being born into a royal family of the correct lineage so that she can assume the throne after the death of the reigning monarch. I can't think of any possible way that you could ever become a queen.

(Silence)

I'm sorry, Lucy, but it's true.

(Silence)

Lucy	...and in the summertime I will go to my summer palace and I'll wear my crown in swimming and everything, and all the people will cheer and I will shout at them. *(She dreams her vision. Then the vision pops.)* What do you mean I can't be a queen?
Linus	It's true.
Lucy	There must be a loophole. This kind of thing always has a loophole. Nobody should be kept from being a queen if she wants to be one. IT'S UNDEMOCRATIC.
Linus	Good grief.
Lucy	It's usually just a matter of knowing the right people. I bet a few pieces of well-placed correspondence and I get to be a queen in no time.

Linus	I think I'll watch television. *(He returns to the set and resumes his watching position.)*
Lucy	I know what I'll do. If I can't be a queen, then I'll be very rich. I'll work and work until I'm very, very rich and then I will buy myself a queendom.
Linus	Good grief.
Lucy	Yes, I'll buy myself a queendom and then I'll kick out the old queen and take over the whole operation myself. I will be head queen. And then all the people…when I go out in my coach all the people will shout at me… *(She glances at the TV, becomes engrossed, crosses to the set. Linus looks at her.)*
Linus	What's the matter, Lucy?
Lucy	Huh?
Linus	What happened to your queendom?
Lucy	Oh that, I've given it up. I've decided to devote my life to cultivating my natural beauty.

PART TWO

MONOLOGUES

THE DAY MY FATHER DIED
BY CARL COHEN

In the following monologue, a boy explores his mixed emotions after the death of his father.

1 Boy
Carl

My father died this morning. I was in the middle of Dr. Strange when my mom told me. She said I could finish my comic but then I had to come into the living room and cry with her and my sister. It wasn't sudden or anything. I knew for a long time that he was dying. We all did. My mom tried to tell me that he was getting better, but I knew it was a lie. See, the thing is, I really didn't want him to get better. He was a much nicer person when he was sick. He didn't have the strength to hit me and he hardly ever yelled anymore. He was sent home from the hospital for awhile, but there were oxygen tanks and syringes all over the house. It was getting kind of ugly so my mom had him sent back. I felt really bad for a long time because the sicker he got, the happier I became. See, he didn't just hit me, he used to beat me up pretty bad, and as he got worse and worse, I got less and less afraid of him. Sometimes, when I was by myself, I even laughed, because I could look into his eyes and I knew he was afraid. I wanted him to feel the way he made me feel.

You know, I really loved him a lot. Even when he was hitting me I loved him. Each time, I thought "after this, everything will be alright." But it never was. I bet he really loved me a lot too. He just didn't know how to show it.

DOG
BY SANDOR WEINER

In this monologue, a boy reveals how he lost both his dog and his father in a very short period of time. The boy's parents are in the process of separating, and his mother is very sad. When the family's beloved dog suddenly dies, things just go from bad to worse.

Disturbed by all the trouble in his life, the boy recounts the series of events that have changed his life forever.

1 Boy

A boy stands in a living room. Evening.

The place smells all clean. Alcohol. In a way, nice. Everyone is looking up at us. A woman with her cat. A man with his poodle. My mother screams, grabs my arm and pulls me outside. "What happened?" I ask her. "What happened?" At home she locks herself in her bedroom. My father sleeps on the couch. "It's just a dog," he tells me. "She'll be okay in the morning." But I can't sleep. I tap on my mother's door. I put my ear up against it. "Mom," I whisper real quiet like. "Mom." She might be asleep. Then I hear a noise. I want to tell my father but he's sleeping.

(Pause)

My father has a new friend. Her name is Michelle. He talks to her on the telephone. My mother can hear. My father tells me, "You'll meet her soon. You'll like her." She wears lipstick and nail polish. I see a mouth opening and fingers.

(Pause)

My mother doesn't make sandwiches. She sits on the couch. Looks at the snapshot in the gold frame. He's licking up the food. His first

208

bowl. Blue. Uhmmmmm. It's good. My mother stares at it all morning. In Social Studies Miss Kinken asks, "How many of you have divorced parents?" I tell her, "My parents still live together, but my mother misses our dog."

(Pause)

Michelle is over for dinner. She's younger than my mother. When Michelle moves I can see alot of her skin. My mother stays in her room while we eat. Michelle touches my father's arm and rubs his leg. "I have to take Michelle home now. Don't wait up."

(Pause)

They leave. I look at the snapshot. I take it out of the frame. I tear it into pieces, burn it with a match and flush it down the toilet. I put my face close to the water.

(Pause)

In the morning my father isn't back. He didn't sleep on the couch. My mother sits there, looking at the white cardboard in the gold frame. She does it for a long time. I make breakfast. Cereal and toast. "Do you want some toast?" I ask my mother. She doesn't look at me. She looks at the cardboard. "He was our dog," she says.

(Pause)

Today I got a postcard from my father. He says Hawaii is very pretty. Michelle likes the beach too. Soon, he says, he'll come and get me.

(Pause)

At night I whisper to myself, "It's just a dog. It's just a dog."

(Lights fade to black.)

FIFTH OF JULY
BY LANFORD WILSON

In the play *Fifth of July*, the flamboyant, theatrical character of Shirley is 14 years old, and bursting with the desire to become a great...*anything!* Shirley feels somewhat stifled in the small Missouri town where she lives, and she yearns to be larger-than-life.

In the following excerpt, Shirley makes a dramatic announcement to her mother (June), her uncle (Ken) and her mother's friends who are visiting from out of town (Gwen and John).

Special Notes
The lines of the other characters in the scene have been printed here in brackets. It may be helpful for the actress playing Shirley to imagine what is being said to her at those places.

1 Girl
Shirley (age 14)

Shirley   *(Quietly determined)* I'm going to be the greatest artist Missouri has ever produced.

[John   Would that be so difficult?]

Shirley   The entire Midwest. What do you mean? There have been very famous people—world-famous people from—Tennessee Williams grew up in (Missouri)—

[John   Tennessee Williams is from Mississippi.]

Shirley   …he grew up…not three blocks from where I live now! All his formative years!

[John   Okay, what do I know.]

Shirley   And Mark Twain. And Dreiser! And Vincent Price and Harry Truman! And Betty Grable!…But me! Oh, God! Me! Me! Me! Me! I am going to be so great! Unqualified! The greatest single artist the Midwest has ever known!

[John   Yes, yes, doing what?]

Shirley   (Doing) Something astonishing! Just astonishing!

[John   In what field? What are you going to be?]

Shirley   A painter. Or a sculptor. Or a dancer! A writer! A conductor! A composer! An actress! One of the arts! People will die. Certain people will literally have cardiac arrests at the magnitude of my achievements.

[John	If you're going to be a dancer or a composer, you might matriculate into some school before too much—]
Shirley	I will have you know that I intend to study for ten years, and then I will burst forth on the world. And people will be abashed!
[Ken	I don't doubt it for a minute.]
Shirley	Amazed!
[Gwen	I think you're terrific.]
Shirley	Astonished! At my magnitude. Oh, God! Look! Is that she? Is that SHE? Is that she? Is it? IT IS! IT IS SHE! IT IS SHE! AHHHHHHHHHHHHH! *(She collapses on the floor.)*
[John	She recognized herself on the street and fainted.]
Shirley	*(Slowly getting to a sitting position; with great dignity.)* She died dead of cardiac arrest and astonishment at the magnificence of my achievement in my chosen field. Only Shakespeare, Michelangelo, Beethoven, and Frank Lloyd Wright have risen to my heights before me....

♀♀♀♀

Shirley	*(To John)* And when I first achieved my first achievements I was eleven years younger than you are now. *(She sweeps to the front door.)*

GAS FOOD LODGING
BY ALLISON ANDERS
BASED ON THE NOVEL,
"DON'T LOOK AND IT WON'T HURT"
BY RICHARD PECK

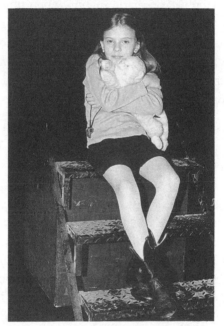

The film *Gas Food Lodging* tells the coming-of-age story of Shade, a young girl growing up in a small town in New Mexico. Abandoned by her father at a very young age, Shade lives with her mother and her older sister in a trailer park. While the three of them love each other very much, Shade's mother, who works as a waitress in a diner, and Shade's sister, Trudi, are always fighting.

Shade often goes alone to the local cinema to forget about her troubles for a while. Her favorite films are the Spanish ones, especially the heart-breaking love stories starring the beautiful, melodramatic actress, *Elvia Rivero*.

In the following excerpt, Shade describes how she became obsessed with the idea of finding a man for her Mom.

1 Girl
Shade

If it weren't for *[the movies of]* **Elvia Rivero**, this story wouldn't even be worth telling. Whenever Elvia[*'s movies*] came to this little town, it's like she woke the place up. My home town, Laramie, New Mexico—it came alive! Elvia Rivero was the one who made me laugh when I needed to laugh...she made me cry when no one was looking... but most of all, Elvia could put into words everything I was thinking. It was Elvia who first gave me the idea: it was decided then and there...I knew what was missing from my life: *a man!* Don't get me wrong, *not* a man for *me*—for my <u>Mom</u>! Then we could do all the dumb, normal stuff *regular* families do.

The question was, what kind of man would my Mom go for? My Dad walked off before I could remember things, and I haven't seen her with any other guy in almost two years...since the one who held the gun on us... Before *him,* there was this really, *really* rich guy, who took me and my sister to K-Mart one day, and let us buy *anything* we wanted... *anything*!!! And we said, "Marry *him,* Mom, Marry him!" But she said no, because if she did it would be for the wrong reason. So that was the end of that. Oh, and then there was this young guy. He was more of a pal. He used to turn off all the lights in our trailer, and go *"BRING ME THE LIGHTS!!! BRING ME THE LIGHTS!!!"*—And me and Trudi would hide in the dark and scream and my Mom would get all mad at him and say : *"Stop it! You're getting them all wound up before bedtime!"* And we'd all laugh so she'd have to laugh. I wonder whatever happened to him...

There's *so* many kinds of guys. There's *so* many kinds. But there's only one guy missing. The man who was missing was John Isiah Perion Evans, My Dad.

I KNOW WHY THE CAGED BIRD SINGS
TELEPLAY BY
LEONORA THUNA AND
MAYA ANGELOU
BASED ON THE NOVEL
"I KNOW WHY THE CAGED BIRD SINGS"
BY MAYA ANGELOU

Originally a novel, *I Know Why the Caged Bird Sings* is the coming-of-age story of Marguerite, a young black girl growing up in the prejudiced South of the 1930s and '40s. For the good part of her childhood, Marguerite lives with her loving grandmother and her uncle in Stamps, Arkansas, where the family runs a dry goods store. Marguerite is brave, intelligent and imaginative but her life is far from easy. Regular threats of violence from the Ku Klux Klan often intimidate her family, and they must be on guard at all times just to stay alive.

The following excerpt takes place at Marguerite's graduation from her segregated, all-black school, the Lafayette Training School. Marguerite has the honor of being the graduation speaker. The mood of the day is joyous and proud, with students, teachers and families all there to celebrate the students' achievements.

Moments before Marguerite makes her speech, however, a white man named Mr. Johnson abruptly interrupts the ceremony. Announcing that he is running for political office, he promises to donate a playing field and a home economic facility to the school if he is elected. Sadly, it is painfully obvious to everyone that he has no regard for the students *or* their school, but rather, that he just wants to buy himself a few votes.

In the face of this indignity, Marguerite changes her graduation speech to suit the situation at hand, and, in doing so, graduates from the Lafayette Training School with much more than just academic honors.

215

1 Girl
Marguerite

Mr. Principal, dear teachers, fellow graduates, and dear parents and friends. Our speaker just told us that he was improving the education facilities in Stamps. He's given us the chance to become basketball players and cooks. Well, I want to thank Mr. Johnson for this chance, but I don't think I'm going to take it. I didn't memorize the whole of *The Rape Of Lucrece* so I could be a cook or a cleaning lady. See, I give Mr. Johnson all the rights he wants, but I don't believe he has the right to decide that my *only* hero has got to be a first line football player. I got other heroes. For example, Edgar Allen Poe because I like what he said, and I liked the way he said it. My teachers, because they showed me a map. And on that map, I saw that the world went past Stamps, Arkansas, United States Of America, North American Continent. And I got another hero…me! And me as not just a proud member of the graduating class of The Lafayette County Training School. Me as a proud member of the Negro race, the wonderful, beautiful Negro race. Well, I'd like to thank Mr. Johnson for the paved playing fields, but I'm not gonna run on it. I got other things to do.

THE JUDI MILLER SHOW
BY MARILYN SUZANNE MILLER

What could be worse than being sent to your room just so your Mom can play her bridge game without any interruptions from *you?*

Well, that's what happens to Judi Miller. Banished to her room with nothing to do, Judi devises a hilarious invention to keep herself entertained: she creates her own imaginary T.V. show! On the fictitious "Judi Miller Show," Judi not only gets to be the star, the announcer, all the supporting characters, cast and crew, but the T.V. commercials, as well! The only problem is, the "show" tends to get faster and wilder and louder and crazier until even Judi's Mom can hear it downstairs—and poor Judi gets in trouble again.

Tune in now, it's time for the "Judi Miller Show"!

1 Girl
Judi

(A girl's bedroom, not unlike the one in "Gidget's Disease." Lots of pink and cuteness. In addition to a bed and dresser, the room must also contain an overstuffed arm chair, a hassock, a large chest that can be stood on at the foot of the bed, several large calico throw pillows and, lined up across the front of the pillows on the bed, a line of dolls and stuffed animals; a Barbie Doll, teddy bear, dog, baby doll, Raggedy Ann, etc. There should be as many as can be humanly stuffed in a line on the bed. Judi enters from a door upstage. She is dressed as a Brownie, wearing your basic Brownie outfit, including socks, beanie, etc. She is yelling out the door.)

O.K., but as soon as your bridge game's over, I'm coming downstairs? *(Slams door.)* I didn't mean to slam it.

(Slams it, makes a face. Stands there for a moment calmly. Then suddenly, throws herself against the door, screams.)

217

I'm so bored! *(Begins jumping on each word, toward her bed.)* Because my room…is…the…boring…room…of…the…world.

(She jumps on her bed, picks her head up opposite the thousands of dolls and stuffed animals, which she gathers in her arms, chanting mindlessly to them, rolling around on her bed, occasionally her head is sticking out from between her legs, above her rear end.)

(Chanting) We are here in my room and this is my room and this is my bed and this is my house and this is my lawn around my house and this is my street and this is my town and this is my country and this is my planet Earth and this is my universe and this is my I don't know and la la la la—

(By this time her head is hanging upside down over the side of the bed. She stops. New sudden determination in her voice.)

—and now, it's time for the Judi Miller Show!

(Jumps up, assembles dolls in her arms on the floor as the audience. Sings to them.)

Oh, it's the show of the day, it's the show of the way, I am in it, oh, yes, I am, oh, it's the show of your life, it's the JU-DI MIL-LER SHOW! Presenting the big famous and you know who it is…star of the show…and here it is—

(Running to bureau drawer, talking to cover while she gets crinoline out which she puts on her head, her back to us.)

—the person who is also a bride named Judi Arlene Miller!

(Turns to face us, big smile, immediately turning into a different character with a big phony English accent.)

Hello. You know, I am the most beautiful person in the whole wide world. *(Sigh, parading around)* Oh, yes, because I am the most beautiful bride anyone has ever seen including everyone in the whole wide world and here comes my husband right now.

(Picks up doll, does doll talking, man's voice) Darling, will you marry me?

(Breathy, sexy bride voice) Yes.

(Takes doll, goes into long, passionate movie kiss. Big phony TV smile.)

And we'll be right back after a word from our sponsor.

(Runs to bed and gets plastic baggie of Saltines she brought into the room with her, holds it up like a product, big smile.)

You know, this is the food which everyone loves because it is the new really good delicious nutritious new thing that is smooth and creamy. *(Takes a bite.)* Mmboy, so when you need a thing that is smooth and creamy, get this and you will really love it, and now, back to the show.

(Smiles, jumps on the bed, starts jumping up and down, sings.)

'Cause it's a show about the person who is jumping up and down so high they can't see, in the sky!

(Leaps off the bed, races to closet, grabs robe, ties it around with the arms tied in the back like a strapless evening gown. English accent.)

And now, presenting The Queen of France.

(Judi begins walking through the room like a queen, talking fake French.)

Oh, je se me larreau, blarreau, zarreau, larue. *(Real fast, rapid fire)* Je te ne se me se ge ge fe fe blareau, zarreau, larreau, darreau, narrow. *(In her regular voice)* But, little does she know that here comes the wicked queen of Germany, Queen…*(Fake German accent)* Dofonoichdorpfo. Oh, no. *(As real mean queen)* Oh yes, and I am going to kill you right now. *(Starts throwing herself against a wall violently.)* Oh, stop, stop killing me. Now we have to run to France. *(Runs from the wall. German voice.)* No! *(Throws self against the wall. French voice.)* We have to run to England. *(Throws self against the wall. German voice.)* No! *(Runs from wall. French voice.)* We have to run to Bolivia. *(Throws self against wall. German voice.)* No! Oh, no. Oh, Queenie, what will we do? I don't know. Well, I do. We'll just kill her starting now.

(Making drum roll noises with her mouth, runs back, jumps on the throw

pillows, the hassock, the chair, the chest, the bed, jumps up and down a few more times, leaps on the floor, lands on all fours.) We smashed her!

(Making all different doll noises, holding each one up, cheering.) Yay, yay, yay, yay.

Mother   *(From offstage)* Judi! What's going on up there?

Judi   *(Quietly)* Nothing.

(Sings, whispering, holds up dolls who sing with her.) Yes, the wonderful bunderful person who is also a ballet dancer... Dah, dah, dah.

Mother   *(From offstage)* Judi, be quiet.

Judi   ...on the Judi Miller Show!

The End

(She somersaults on to the bed.)

(Fade out)

LETTERS TO AN ALIEN
BY ROBERT CAISLEY

When twelve-year-old Hannah is forced to stay with her Grandfather, "Pops," she doesn't want to. There's something unspoken about her Grandfather, a Jewish artist from the old country, that makes Hannah nervous, even angry. But Hannah's parents have insisted that she stay with Pops, in order to "learn something" important from him.

The visit begins badly. Hannah is only interested in playing video games, while Pops wants Hannah to sit still so he can paint her portrait. As they spend more time alone together, however, Hannah and her Grandfather begin to take steps towards understanding one another, and a sort of healing is able to take place.

In the following speech, Hannah confronts Pops with a painful secret from his past.

Special Notes
Pop's lines in the scene have been printed here in brackets. It may be helpful for the actress playing Hannah to imagine what is being said to her at those places.

1 Girl
Hannah (age 12)

Hannah   I was wrong, we're not Aliens, we're exactly the same you and I. Forwards and backwards. Inside and out. We both hate so much what we are.

[Pops   I don't hate. I don't. It's other people.]

Hannah   No, Poppa. It's all of us. That's what we have to learn. That we're all capable of hating, hurting, and even killing.

[Pops reaches out to grab the paintings from her; she won't let go. She holds onto his arm and rolls his sleeve up to reveal the tattooed number.]

Please, Poppa, don't hide it. Don't hide your life in a painting. 772 2736.

[Pops   What...did you call me?]

Hannah   772 2736. I've seen it before. That mark on your arm. 772 2736. When I was little, I told my friend about it, and we laughed, Poppa. We laughed at you. We made jokes that you were a robot and that was your special code number. But all the time I was laughing something inside told me, it's no joke. I was so scared that number meant you were different and I didn't want to be like you. Every morning I'd check my arms...I thought a number might suddenly appear. *(Beat)* What I've seen in books, your arm, your songs, these paintings...it's just little bits and pieces. A jig-saw puzzle I'm trying to put together, but people keep stealing the pieces. *(Beat)* In class I have to talk about something that's important to me, and I've found out what's important. My history and you, Poppa. Will you help me?

LITTLE RICKY
BY ARTHUR T. WILSON

In this next monologue, a boy named Ricky describes a valuable lesson that he learned from his mother about the importance of fighting back.

1 Boy
Ricky

When I was three years old, I wanted to buy a birthday present for my brother, who was five. I didn't want to ask my parents for the money, so I broke into my piggy bank, where I had saved some money from errands and allowances. I asked my mother to take me to the shopping mall. At the shopping mall, we looked at many toys. Finally, I found a truck that I knew my brother would like because he had seen the same truck at a friend's house and went, *"Oh, wow! Isn't this great?!"* So, we were going to buy the truck. When the man in the store took the truck down from the shelf, I pulled out my brown bag of pennies and put them on the counter. He was very nasty, and refused to take the money if it wasn't wrapped in those coin papers that you get at the bank. My mother explained to him that it was for a birthday gift for my brother, but he didn't want to hear it. He immediately asked us, *"Are you going to pay in dollars or what? If not, I have other things to do."* My mother smiled, put my money back in the bag, and we left the store. I was confused but knew that I was going to get my brother a birthday gift.

That weekend, my mother wrote a letter to the editor of our community newspaper, and explained how we were treated at the store. Several days later, my mother got a telephone call from the shopkeeper and he told her that we could come back to the store and buy the truck for my brother.

MANCHILD IN THE PROMISED LAND
BY CLAUDE BROWN

Manchild in the Promised Land is the autobiography of Claude Brown. Claude began his life as a juvenile delinquent but eventually became a college graduate and a renowned author. As a youngster growing up in Harlem, Claude grew up fast and got into trouble at a young age, cutting school, stealing and even building guns. Often he would run away from home, staying away for weeks at a time. As a result of this behavior, Claude was taken to various children's centers, from which—again—he would always manage to run away. Eventually, however, Claude managed to find the strength to turn his life around, get a college degree and write his remarkable life-story.

In the following section, Claude talks about his early love of the streets.

1 Boy
Claude

I used to feel that I belonged on the Harlem streets and that, regardless of what I did, nobody had any business to take me off the streets.

I remember when I ran away from shelters, places that they sent me to, here in the city. I never ran away with the thought in mind of coming home. I always ran away to get back to the streets. I always thought of Harlem as home, but I never thought of Harlem as being in the house. To me, home was the streets. I suppose there were many people who felt that. If home was so miserable, the street was the place to be. I wonder if mine was really so miserable, or if it was that there was so much happening out in the street that it made home seem such a dull and dismal place.

When I was very young—about five years old, maybe younger—I would always be sitting out on the stoop. I remember Mama telling

224

me and Carole to sit on the stoop and not to move away from in front of the door. Even when it was time to go up and Carole would be pulling on me to come upstairs and eat, I never wanted to go, because there was so much out there in that street.

You might see somebody get cut or killed. I could go out in the street for an afternoon, and I would see so much that, when I came in the house, I'd be talking and talking for what seemed like hours. Dad would say, "Boy, why don't you stop that lyin'? You know you didn't see all that. You know you didn't see nobody do that." But I knew I had.

THE ME NOBODY KNOWS
EDITED BY
STEPHEN M. JOSEPH
MONOLOGUE BY "RONALD C."

The Me Nobody Knows is a collection of poetry and prose written by children between the ages of 7-18 attending the New York City public schools in Bedford-Stuyvesant, Harlem, Jamaica, Manhattan, and the Youth House in the Bronx. The book was so successful that eventually it was made into a Broadway musical.

In the following monologue, one student, Ronald, describes how he is always getting into trouble.

Special Notes
Ronald's reference to the seventh grade can be changed to suit the age of the actor, if necessary.

1 Boy
Ronald

My parents hardly never understand my problems because sometimes i will get in trouble like on April fool day. i would tell a teacher her toes are bleeding and then i'll get in trouble, when i would be only fooling around and then my mother would have to come to school and then i'll get a beating, and i'll try to make her understand it was a joke like anyone would do.

One of the teaches in this school he's a man. When he be walking in the halls he would tap me on my shoulder and when i was in the 7th grade two years from now i tapped this teacher on the shoulder. I was just playing and he went down to the principal and tell them i gave him a CARATE Chop Chop and then i got in trouble right then.

My mother had to come to school and a lot of crap. And i tried to explain to her i was just playing with the teacher. But she just didn't believe me. She think that i can't do nothing by myself.

MEN DON'T LEAVE
SCREENPLAY
BY BARBARA BENEDEK
AND PAUL BRICKMAN

The film *Men Don't Leave* tells the story of Beth, a Maryland housewife, who is unexpectedly widowed when her husband is killed in a freak accident at work. Left with two sons and little money, she sells her beautiful suburban home in order to take an apartment in the city of Baltimore, where she can find a job.

The two boys have more than their share of adjusting to do. They must not only deal with the sudden death of their father, but also with the move from their safe suburban neighborhood to a large, not-so-friendly city. With their mother now working full-time, they are forced to become more independent and learn how to take care of themselves. And then there is their mother's new boyfriend, *Charles*...a free-spirited musician who isn't anything like their father was.

Chris, the oldest son, resents his Mom's new boyfriend and is hostile to him. Beth eventually does break up with Charles, but not on account of her son's behavior. She has been through so much loss in such a short period of time, that she is simply not ready for a whole new relationship. Beth goes into a state of withdrawal, unable to leave the apartment.

When Chris sees how depressed his mother has become, he gets really scared. He blames himself for the fact that she is all alone. He goes to see Charles, and, in the following excerpt, tries to convince him to go out with his mom once again.

Special Notes
Please note where Charles' lines appear in brackets. It may be helpful for the actor playing Chris to imagine what is being said to him at those places.

1 Boy
Chris

Chris   Hi.

[Charles   Hey Chris.]

Chris   Did I borrow this album from you?

[Charles   I don't think so.]

Chris   That's so weird. I wonder whose it could be.

[Charles   Chris, is everything alright?]

Chris   ...Is there a place we could talk? ... Are you and my mother still friends?

[Charles   I think we are.]

Chris   Because you don't come around too much anymore.

[Charles   Yes. That's true. But I hope I can still think of her as my friend.]

Chris   *(Pitching his heart out.)* You can. You definitely can. And she's a good friend to have. She's very loyal and has a good personality. Everybody likes her. Everybody that knows her.

[Charles   She's a terrific person, your mom.]

Chris   She really is. She's great. So how come you don't come around any more? I'm sure there must be a real good reason.

[Charles   It's a little complicated to explain, Chris.]

Chris   *(Intense)* I know I haven't been very nice to you some of the time, but it's not that I don't like you. It's not that. It just takes me a while to get used to new people. But then when I do, I'm really friendly. I can be a lot of fun.

[**Charles**   Chris. This doesn't have anything to do with you. You were fine. I don't want you to think…]

Chris   *(Rushing to get this out.)* I wasn't fine. I know that. I'm sorry. I apologize. I can be different if you just give me a chance. You and I could be friends and get along and I'll go to classical musical concerts whenever you want. And I could even do some things around the house for you. I could mow your lawn if you ever grow one because you see, my mother really likes having you as a friend. She doesn't really know a lot of people here and I think she's getting sad again, and when she had you to talk to she didn't seem so sad and I know I was a real pain in the ass and I promise I won't be and I know you probably don't believe me, but maybe if you could just give me another chance. Cause I — *(faltering, voice breaking)* — I really hate to see her so lonely.

THE NEW AMERICANS
BY ELIZABETH SWADOS

The New Americans explores the changing ethnic identities of the families currently immigrating to the United States. A musical portrait of youngsters from Asia, India, Africa and South America, *The New Americans* dramatizes the journey such children must take to get to America, and also the frightening, often confusing transition they must make after they uproot themselves from one culture and settle into the next.

In the play, some of the children have come to America for better education and opportunities; others have fled from countries besieged by war; still others were encouraged by parents who wanted a better future for their families. Whatever their differences, *all* of the youngsters share a strong desire to fit into the American way of life. Using story, drama, dance and song, *The New Americans* explores some of the expectations, the disappointments and the survival tactics of contemporary immigrant children as they struggle to adapt to a whole new world.

In the following monologue, Derdre, of Trinidadian background, describes some of the difficulty her family encounters once they arrive in America.

1 Girl
Derdre

One lady knew another and the ladies help each other and my Mama got a name of some white family on Sixty-Third Street and Park Avenue and now she's their maid. This apartment looks like a fancy doll house. Everything's pillows and carpets and curves. Since nobody's ever home I don't know what gets dirty, but everyday my Mama changes into her white uniform and vacuums the carpets, waxes the wood and linoleum, dust the shelves of books, make the beds, picks up the toys, washes out the laundry and prepares the kitchen so the cook can begin the meals. The family has so many jobs and houses and activities my Mama says they do everything but live. I'm worried about her. Mama's blood pressure's going up in this heat. She misses her house on the island. She doesn't want to flush anyone's toilet but her own. My Papa says, "Quit, quit. The little ones are growing up without you." "I want a house in the mountains," my Mama says. "A tree, a rock, a stream and some golden fish." Last night she came home with a present from the rich lady. A pink brocade cotton sweater with Atlantic City printed on its pockets. My Mama pulled it on over her uniform, drank a half a bottle of Sunshine Liquor and fell asleep in her chair. Papa went off somewhere. I don't know where.

RUSHING WATERS
BY MIGDALIA CRUZ

Rushing Waters is a musical portraying the history of a town in California, called *Pocoima*. In the play, history and fantasy unite, and magical spirits watch over even the town's most mistreated inhabitants.

In the following monologue, Kooka, who is half-Mexican, half-Puerto Rican, tells how she tried to hide her mixed ethnic identity in order to be accepted. When she finds a boyfriend in the rebellious, tough-talking *C.K. Ice,* she finds the courage to be true to herself. Tragically, C.K. is shot by a policeman one night, and Kooka is ripped apart by the loss. But even after C.K. is gone, Kooka's can't stop the expression of her own identity from flowing out of her.

1 Girl
Kooka

I used to tell people my grandmother was from San Luis Potosi. The real one. I saw it on some bubble gum—you know, that Canel gum. That's where they make it, I guess. Sounded pretty—like a waterfall. You know that "poooh" sound in "pooohtoohsi" and all. And anyways it was in Mexico…And I was half-Mexican. But I din't know from where because my Papi died before I even knew him and his folks never wanned nuffin to do wif my Ma because she was Puerto Rican and me—because I spoke weird Spanish and I weren't one hundred percent…

It worked for a while. For awhile I passed—I was like family, but then…I don' know. I jus' started talking like I talk—like I talk for real. I mean, it was like I couldn't help myself. My Puerto Rican side came out—after I met C.K.…That's when I got the courage. I just stopped hiding myself. I stopped caring about what other people thought and then, well, I jus'started talking. And when I talk it comes outta me like a rush of water. It comes pouring—my words. Tripping on themselves—

233

too fast. Too fast. I drown myself with them. I'm drowning 'cause I'm not a part of this place. It don't let me be.

(Pause)

When Ice was history, I jus' couldn't stop talkin'.* …When I talk it comes outta me like a rush of water. It comes pouring—my words. Tripping on themselves—too fast. I drown… I drown. I'm tripping—on my words. I'm tripping… It's like a rush of water.

---

* "Ice" is C.K.'s other nickname.

SAMMY CARDUCCI'S GUIDE TO WOMEN
BY RONALD KIDD

In the play, *Sammy Carducci's Guide to Women,* an eleven-year-old expert on women, Samuele Lorenzo Carducci (better known as "Sammy") finds out that girls are people, too.

Before he delivers this monologue, Sammy and his best friend, Gus, are in the school cafeteria conducting a survey on—*what else?*—women! *(See earlier scene on page 135.)* When Sammy spots Becky, a sixth-grader, however, he falls in love at first sight, and his survey is finished forever.

1 Boy
Sammy (age 12)

…So I'm standing there in the cafeteria, doing my survey with Gus, when all of a sudden I'm staring at the most gorgeous woman I've ever seen. She looks fourteen or fifteen at least, but I know she couldn't be, because my school only goes up to the sixth grade. At first I think maybe she flunked a grade or two. Then I look at her eyes, which shine like a couple of spotlights, and I know she's too smart for that. While I'm watching, she pushes her hair back behind one ear and smiles. I get this incredible feeling, like…how can I explain it? It's like somebody ran one of those rubber squeegees across the windshield of my life. Kinda poetic, huh? I get like that sometimes. Suddenly everything's bright and clear. I know without a doubt she is the woman of my dreams.

That afternoon I check around and find out some key facts about her. Turns out her name is Becky Davidson, and she's in Mr. Lawrence's sixth-grade class. She's smart, and she loves to read. She works in the library with her skinny friend, Alice Biddle. So, when class is over, Gus and I *[will]* head over there.

SKIN
BY DENNIS FOON

The play, *Skin,* explores the lives of three different children living in Canada: Phirozoa, from Bombay, Karen, of Native American origin, and Tuan, a recent immigrant from North Vietnam. The play interweaves their separate stories as each youngster struggles with the need to embrace their own cultural identity.

In the following monologue, Tuan describes how he made the terrifying journey all the way from Vietnam to Canada in a small boat.

1 Boy
Tuan

My name is Wong Tuan Hung [*pronounced: Wun Hungh Dwon*]. In Chinese, my name means many things. I was born in Hanoi, North Vietnam. My father is Chinese, my mother Vietnamese. When the conflict started between China and Vietnam, it was very hard for us to live. My parents thought it would be safer if we left the country for a while but they only had enough money to send my older brother, younger sister and me. My parents stayed behind.

When we left Vietnam there were 300 of us in a thirty meter boat. It was pretty crowded. When half of us slept, the other half stood to make room. We floated for over half a month. We kept asking ships from different countries to tow us to the mainland but they wouldn't get involved. Besides, they said, we weren't in any danger—the boat was still floating. But then it sank, so we were given help. About sixty people drowned, though. Including my older brother.

†††††

We were taken to Hong Kong where we stayed in a camp with other refugees. It was hard in the camp. Many people were cruel to us because they thought we were Vietnamese. But we left Vietnam because they were hard on us for being Chinese. Sometimes it is very difficult to understand the way people behave...But then a church in Canada sponsored us and we came to Vancouver. When we first came off the plane, our sponsors were there to meet us. But no one spoke Chinese or Vietnamese so it was very confusing.

But our sponsors were very nice. They really wanted to help. But we were quite confused. Their house was different from any we had ever seen. And the food was strange. Our first day of school we were given lunch boxes. *(He holds up a ridiculous lunch box.)* It seemed like an odd way to carry food.

English classes take place in an annex outside the school.

My sponsors helped me find work. Every night and on weekends I would clean office buildings. It was hard to do that and study for school too, but I had to send money to my parents. They wanted to leave Vietnam to come and be with us. And I needed money so my sister and I could eat...

Sometimes late at night when I am mopping floors, I stop and listen. The empty building, so hollow. Buzzing of florescent tubes. Outside rain beats against windows. I feel...like I'm underwater. I think: around the corner, my brother will be standing. Waiting to grab the mop from my hands, shouting, "You're my little brother, why are you working when you should be sleeping? Give that mop to me, that is my job!" And I look at him, and his hair is still wet, wet like it was the last time I saw him. I want to say, "Did you swim, I thought you drowned. How did you find me here, in Canada, in this city, in this building right now? You didn't drown, you're alive and you made it all the way to me."

...And I walk down the corridor, turn the corner and look. The hallway goes on forever. It's so empty. No sound but the hum of lights. And the rain against the windows.

SPINE
BY BILL C. DAVIS

In the play *Spine*, a fragmented family comes together on the last night of their youngest son's life. Set in a Connecticut country home, *Spine* explores the family's struggle to cope with the illness of their youngest son, *Christy*. With the illness in an advanced state, Christy is unable to speak or move. He can only communicate by blinking his eyes "yes" or "no."

When Claire, Christy's older sister, is told that Christy may not live until his next birthday, she decides to give him his birthday present early. It is scary for Claire to do this, because it means that she acknowledges that Christy will die soon. In the following monologue, Claire finds the words to say good-bye to her brother forever.

1 Girl
Claire

It's really weird that you can't talk. But I know what you want to say. I do. You want to say, "Claire—you're a very good sister." And I want to say, "You're a very good brother"—you are, Christy. You're a better brother than Mike. I guess that's not saying very much. Charlene and Reesy and Jenny ask about you. They worry about you. They worry that you're having pain, cause I told them when I've heard you yell. I didn't tell them when you cried—I wouldn't do that. But a few times you screamed. The first time you did that, I was so scared. It was the most scared I've ever been until just a little while ago—until just before I gave you your present. *That* was the most scared I've ever been. But that's not my secret. *(Pause)* I thought something awful once—not too long ago. Remember July fourth? You wanted us to go to the lake and I wanted us to go to the ocean, because they have the best fireworks; they shoot them from the boats and you can see them in the sky and in the water—like stereo. But you wanted to go fishing in the lake. I was real mad, you know. You throw the fish back anyway. But I was so mad, because that's what always happens. Whenever you want to go somewhere that's where we always go. And I wished something awful—I was wrong—I know I was, but I wished... I said to myself, "I wish he'd hurry up and..."

(She can't say it)

It was bad to think that, and I really didn't think it long. I just wanted to see the fireworks from the boats. And that's not what I wish. I wish you'd never die. That's what I really wish, Christy. I'm sorry. Blink that you forgive me.

(Christy blinks)

Thanks Christy.

(Claire kisses him. She leaves his bed and goes....)

TELLING TALES
BY MIGDALIA CRUZ

Many of the stories told in the play, *Telling Tales,* describe the experiences of young Puerto Rican girls and women living in the inner city. In the following monologue, the speaker describes her changing relationship with her first love, *Papo Chibirico.*

1 Girl

Papo Chibirico was fifteen when I was seven. He was my first love. He bought me coloring books and candy and took me to the zoo. Anthony Vargas tried to give me coloring books too, but I punched him in the nose and made him bleed. Papo thought it was a good idea. "Don't let the boys bully you," he always said.

Every summer we formed softball teams. Once we were playing and I walked backwards to make a catch. I didn't know I was on a hill and fell off into a pile of beer bottles. Papo carried me the fifteen blocks home with one hand holding my left knee together. He pulled the glass out of the wound and went with my Mom and me to the hospital. He was mature for a kid. That's what I thought.

When I turned eleven, I went to P.R. for the summer. I returned a foot and a half taller and five shades darker. Papo was six inches shorter than me then. How could he be six inches shorter, if he was eight years older? Papo changed that summer too, he got more muscles and was training to become a wrestler. My Dad and I watched his first televised fight on Channel forty-seven. That's when I found out he was a midget—because he was a midget wrestler.

Papo fought the Jamaican Kid. The strength was in their arms really. Their little legs just kicked the air. With their arms they pinned each other to the floor. My Dad laughed and I wondered what was so funny. He explained to me that it was supposed to be funny—that's why you watch midget wrestling, to laugh. The Jamaican Kid won.

The next day I saw Papo. He was still friendly to me even though he was a TV star. All the kids on the block wanted to talk to him. But he talked just to me. The big kids were always challenging him to a fight. He would say "No," but they would push him and hit him until there was nothing left to say. Sometimes three or four would gang up on him and hold him up in the air. His useless legs would swing wildly at his attackers always missing their mark. "Some tough guy!" Then they'd throw him into a dumpster. I used to watch and cry because I didn't know what else to do. All I could do was wait for them to leave and help Papo out of the garbage. He always got mad at me then. "Don't you know you could get hurt?! Stay away from me, will you! I don't need your help!" But he always needed my help.

He got to be a really good wrestler. The kind the crowd stands up for. He got tougher too. Carried a knife and stabbed somebody, so I couldn't see him anymore. He'd look at me from across the street when I was sitting on the fire escape doing my homework. He waved and I waved back, but he always turned away before he saw me wave. I guess he was afraid I wouldn't.

When he got a little money saved, he got a special bicycle on which he could reach the pedals. He spent hours on that bike, circling the neighborhood. I watched him go by and go by and go by again. He looked normal on that bike—happy. He walked with a limp now. The Jamaican Kid went crazy one night and bit a chunk out of his calf. He got an infection from it. The Jamaican Kid never even apologized. I know because I asked. That's the last thing we ever talked about.

It was one of those real hot August nights, when everybody's on the street because nobody can sleep. Some guys are playing the congas in the playground, small children are playing tag, mothers are gossiping and the men are playing dominoes. Papo comes by on his bike. It's a pretty one—black with a red seat and Papo's in red and black too. He looks sharp. His face is pretty. He's the only one on the block with green eyes. Everybody wanted those eyes. Everybody says hello. He starts showing off, making the bike jump and taking turns real fast and low. People applaud. He does this over and over, people finally stop watching but he keeps saying "Look at me, look at me." Now people are embarrassed to look. Papo goes by one more time...

I don't know where the car came from. It was a new car, I think. Shiny. Maybe just freshly waxed. People always wax their cars in the summer. He wouldn't have lived long anyway—that's what people said. "God bless him. Midgets don't live very long."

But he wasn't a midget, he was a dwarf.

THANK YOU AND GOODNIGHT
SCREENPLAY BY JAN OXENBERG

A filmmaker looks back on her relationship with her Grandmother in these excerpts from her documentary-style film, *Thank You and Goodnight*.

1 Girl
Jan

My Grandmother died a couple years ago, and I find myself still looking for her. I keep thinking I see her purse, or her dress or her shoes... When I told people my Grandmother was sick, they would always say, "Were you very close?" and I would say, "No." But I still can't seem to accept her death. Okay, I know it's not healthy, but I'm not giving up.

When I was five years old, my Grandmother took me to Paradise. *The* Paradise, that is. The biggest movie palace around. But I wasn't scared. I was with Grandma. She was a big presence in my life back then. I felt like she was all around me. Not that I was nice to her or anything. Not that I let her think I was having a good time. I was a scowling little kid. But then, Grandma and I understood each other.

ᛉᛉᛉᛉ

Learning was very important in my family. When I was little, I was interested in astronomy, the dangers of asteroids... which stars are the oldest...what *"light years"* means.... Grandma was always trying to show me off to her friends, saying things like, "Tell them how far the moon is from the earth, Jan." "No!" I was a rotten kid. I didn't want to make Grandma happy. And anyway, I forgot the answer.

ᛉᛉᛉᛉ

243

I remember when Grandma took me to Coney Island. We had a great time on the rides. The tilt-a-whirl, spider, bumper cars, the cyclone, the whip. I tried to win a stuffed animal. I almost got lost. I was so scared. I couldn't find her anywhere, but I tried to pretend to myself that I was still having fun. Everybody looked like her, but nobody was her. I was scared I wouldn't find her, and then I'd be lost.

⛄⛄⛄⛄

(Right after Grandma died), my mother said we should make a list of things to do to help us get through the next few days. I must have heard her wrong—I made a list of things I *didn't* do. I *didn't* help Grandma buy shelves for her salt and pepper shaker collection; I *didn't* call her on her birthday; I never really showed her what she meant to me…If I could just see her one more time, I wouldn't waste it.

⛄⛄⛄⛄

I wish I could make my own apartment. I wish I could keep all her things together. Just the way they were. Just the way she had them. I wouldn't cart her things off. I'd keep one place on earth just the way Grandma made it. I'd have her chair, and her bed, and her pictures… and I could go there and visit Grandma, forever. But if I made my own apartment, which Grandma would I put in it?…the sick Grandma moaning and dying in bed?…the lonely Grandma, who sat in her room day after day and night after night, with no one to talk to and no one to visit her?…the Grandma who was scared to go to sleep at night so she stayed up and played solitaire? If I put Grandma in the room, would she have to die over and over again? Why can't things just stay the way they are? Why do people have to die anyway?

⛄⛄⛄⛄

Occasionally, I have a dream with Grandma in it, but for the most part, things are pretty much back to normal. But I still wish I could see her one more time.

244

THAT NIGHT
SCREENPLAY BY CRAIG BOLOTIN
BASED ON THE NOVEL "THAT NIGHT"
BY ALICE MCDERMOTT

Set in a Long Island suburb in the early 1960s, the film *That Night* portrays the relationship between Alice, a young girl, and her next door neighbor, Sheryl. Sheryl is beautiful, in her teens, and magnetically attractive to boys. Alice admires and idolizes Sheryl, and tries to be like her in every possible way.

Over the course of one summer, however, Alice watches her friend's life change from better to worse as Sheryl goes through a series of painful experiences: the death of her father, a torrid romance with a boy who meets with her mother's disapproval, and finally, pregnancy. When Sheryl is shipped off to a home for unwed teenaged mothers, Alice does everything she can to help keep the lines of communication open between Sheryl and her boyfriend, who has been barred from visiting or even writing to Sheryl. In trying to help Sheryl, Alice takes many risks, and, by the end of the summer, Alice has changed, too. She has learned about life and about love.

1 Girl
Alice (age 11)

It was the summer everyone thought that the Russians were going to invade Long Island any minute, and President Kennedy was going to Berlin to head them off. Sputnik had been around the world ten times, and Mr. Rossi, our neighbor swore he saw it fly right over his back yard. But I had other things on my mind that summer, and so did everyone else on my block.

The Meyer twins were always fighting about something. They'd do just about anything to get [*my friends'*] Cathryn's and Barbara's attention. They were always teasing me. Nicki was the worst. Once, behind the Rossi house, he said he wanted to kiss me—then he spit in my ear.

...I read everything I could about love. Like "MODERN ROMANCE," Encyclopedias, even stuff that took a whole month to get in the mail. But still, I felt like it was some big secret everyone was in on but me. Except sometimes, late at night, when Sheryl came home.

Right after she moved in last winter, the boys started coming around. They all wanted her to go steady, and be their girl. But she wasn't interested...

...If I could just be her for one night...even for just one minute...

I found out *everything* about her...that she played the same song every night, "RULER OF MY HEART." I knew that every Friday, after school, she bought a brand new scarf at Woolworth's...that she put

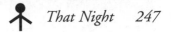

her favorite perfume on every night before she went to sleep...it was "Ambush"—that she thought Brenda Lee was alright, because she turned down a date with Ricky Nelson, and that JFK was the coolest Catholic she knew—outside of her Dad...and that a nun at Mount Saint Mary's slapped her in the face with all her might, and she didn't even cry...that she never slept in anything at all, even in the middle of winter.

She didn't know me, or my name...but I wanted to laugh her laugh and dream her dreams.

The Russians never did invade Long Island, and Mr. Rossi turned out to be all wrong about seeing Sputnik flying over his back yard. But I learned some things that summer...things I'd never forget.

TV MAGIC
BY JOHN L. BADER

In this short monologue, a small boy reveals his future plans.

1 Boy
John

How could they do it? How could they schedule a test this week of all weeks? I mean it's the new fall TV lineup! I just don't understand why they had to decide that school should start every year just as all the new TV shows are starting up as well. Don't the teachers want to watch all the new shows, too?

Do you believe there are kids whose parents won't let them watch TV? How can you *live* and *not* watch TV? Don't people realize that TV is magic? You can go anywhere you want inside a TV screen. It could be the jungles of Africa with Tarzan. It could be the Wild West. You could be trapped in a submarine with only minutes of air left. Fighting in the trenches along with your buddies. And the best thing of all is that no one gets hurt. It's all safe. They're all just having fun inside that little box. And they get paid for it, too. Some day I want to be inside that little box, having fun and getting paid. That's why I want to be an actor. I wish life were a lot more like TV.

WHITE MAGIC
BY ALEXIS GEORGIOU
AGE 11
(DEDICATED TO THE MEMORY OF
PUSS 'N' BOOTS)

White Magic, was written by one of the students in my class. The story is about an eleven year old girl, named Melissa, who has cancer. Melissa goes through many emotions, as she copes with her life-threatening disease.

In the following monologue, Melissa describes the different ways that people treat her once they learn that she is terminally ill.

1 Girl
Melissa (age 11)

My name is Melissa Leah Lakow, I'm 11 years old and I have cancer.

When I first found out that I had leukemia, I couldn't accept it. How could I have cancer? Me, who never even stands in front of the microwave? *Me,* whose Mother always insists on my having suntan lotion on? *Me,* who has never even been in a hospital except when I was born? Why do *I,* of all the people in the world, have leukemia? My parents took it worse, neither of them could believe that their "little girl" had cancer. My Mom keeps trying to make everything up to me because "when you have cancer, one thing you don't have is any fun." My Dad is kind of hard to explain, he treats me as if I *am* the disease rather then I have it. He's not really mean, though. I know that he doesn't want to hurt me, he's just scared. My friends haven't come to visit me yet, but I've only been in the hospital a week. The nurses are friendly. So are the Doctors but they never really stay and talk. My favorite nurse's name is Kelsey Komers. She always treats me as a normal human being, which is really what I am.

WOMEN AND WALLACE
BY JONATHAN MARC SHERMAN

The play, *Women and Wallace* is about Wallace, a boy who loses his mother at a very young age. Throughout his life, he has to learn how to cope with the death of his Mom—a woman who he loved very much.

In the following excerpt, Wallace reads a homework assignment aloud to his class at school. At this point in the play, his mother is still alive.

1 Boy
Wallace (age 6)

"Mommy." By Wallace Kirkman. Age Six. I love Mommy because she makes me peanut butter and banana sandwiches on Wonder bread and it tastes better than when I order it at a restaurant. And Mommy never looks at me funny like the waiters in restaurants do. And Mommy crushes aspirins and mixes them into jelly when I get sick. Because I can't swallow aspirins. They just sit on my tongue and wait for me to finish the whole glass of water. And then I spit them out. But when they're mixed into jelly, I hardly have any problem at all. I just eat the jelly and feel better. And Mommy washes my clothes, so I don't have to. And she does it so they all smell nice when they come out. They come out smelling clean. And they even smell a little like Mommy, because she folds them for me, and her smell rubs off onto my shirts. She smells like perfume. Not really sweet, like Billy Corkscraw's mother. Mommy smells like she's getting ready to go out to dinner. And Mommy's read every book in the library downstairs. I couldn't do that. She can read three books in a week with no trouble at all. Real books, not *"The Hardy Boys."* Mommy's really smart. She can read and take care of me. Both. That's why I love Mommy.

ZLATA'S DIARY
A CHILD'S LIFE IN SARAJEVO
BY ZLATA FILIPOVIC

A young Bosnian girl, Zlata Filipovic has been called the *"Anne Frank"* of Sarajevo. Like Anne Frank, Zlata was eleven years old when she first began keeping a diary, which she named *Mimmy*. When she began her diary, Zlata was leading a normal, happy life. An only child, her father was a lawyer and her mother, a chemist. Together, the three lived comfortably and happily in their elegant apartment in the beautiful city of Sarajevo.

Just months after Zlata began her diary, however, war broke out all around her. Barricades went up in her city, and heavy shelling began. Many people that Zlata knew were hurt—sadly, many were killed. Her family survived for over two years with barely any electricity, heat, water or food. When firing occurred, they would huddle in their cellar for protection. They lived in fear and desperation until they were able to escape to Paris with the help of the UN.

In the following journal entry, Zlata expresses some of her feelings about the war and the need for peace.

Special Notes
It is interesting to read or perform this excerpt from *Zlata's Diary* along with excerpts from *The Diary of Anne Frank.*

1 Girl
Zlata (age 11)

Saturday, May 2, 1992

Today was truly, absolutely the worst day ever in Sarajevo. The shooting started around noon. Mommy and I moved into the hall. Daddy was in his office, under our apartment, at the time. We told him on the intercom to run quickly to the downstairs lobby where we'd meet him. We brought *[my canary]* Cicko with us. The gunfire was getting worse, and we couldn't get over the wall to the Bobars', so we ran down to our own cellar.

The cellar is ugly, dark, smelly. Mommy, who's terrified of mice, had two fears to cope with. The three of us were in the same corner as the other day. We listened to the pounding shells, the shooting, the thundering noise overhead. We even heard planes. At one moment I realized that this awful cellar was the only place that could save our lives. Suddenly, it started to look almost warm and nice. It was the only way we could defend ourselves against all this terrible shooting. We heard glass shattering in our street. Horrible. I put my fingers in my ears to block out the terrible sounds. I was worried about Cicko. We had left him behind in the lobby. Would he catch cold there? Would something hit him? I was terribly hungry and thirsty...

At around 8:00 we went back up to our apartment. Almost every window in our street was broken. Ours were all right, thank God. I saw the post office in flames. A terrible sight... The place is knee-deep in glass.

We're worried about Grandma and Granddad… Tomorrow, if we can go out, we'll see how they are. A terrible day. This has been the worst, most awful day in my eleven-year-old life. I hope it will be the only one… Ciao!
Zlata

This next journal entry was written by Zlata more than half a year later.

Thursday, November 19, 1992.

…I keep wanting to explain these stupid politics to myself, because it seems to me that politics caused this war, making it our everyday reality… It looks to me as though these politics mean Serbs, Croats and Muslims. But they are all people. They are all the same. They all look like people, there's no difference. They all have arms, legs and heads, they walk and talk, but now there's "something" that wants to make them different.

Among my girlfriends, among our friends in our family, there are Serbs and Croats and Muslims. It's a mixed group and I never knew who was a Serb, a Croat or a Muslim. Now politics has started meddling around. It has put an "S" on Serbs, an "M" on Muslims and a "C" on Croats, it wants to separate them. And to do so it has chosen the worst, blackest pencil of all—the pencil of war which spells only misery and death.

Why is politics making us unhappy, separating us, when we ourselves know who is good and who isn't? We mix with the good, not with the bad. And among the good there are Serbs and Croats and Muslims, just as there are among the bad. I simply don't understand it. Of course, I'm "young," and politics are conducted by "grown-ups." But I think we "young" would do it better. We certainly wouldn't have chosen war…

A bit of philosophizing on my part, but I was alone and felt I could write this to you, Mimmy. You understand me. Fortunately, I've got you to talk to. And now,

Love, Zlata

PLAYWRITING
IN THE SCHOOLS

The following monologues were written by children from The Playwriting in the Schools (PITS) program at the Joseph Papp Public Theater at the New York Shakespeare Festival. The program, now in its eleventh year is being conducted under the leadership of Director Arthur T. Wilson and Associate Director Nefretete S. Rasheed. PITS is an arts and literacy empowerment program that provides workshops for regional and international residencies and schools; as well as outreach programs for local community agencies including Children Living in Temporary Housing, hospitals, mental health clinics, colleges and universities.

During PITS workshops, students are introduced to the fundamentals of playwriting and drama. The workshops are structured as an organic and "alive" invitation to action and participation. Students are led through the process by way of theater games, improvisation, conflict resolution and values clarification exercises. Students learn in an atmosphere of creativity and discovery where there are no creative rights and wrongs and are given an opportunity to follow their intuitive hunches in a charged atmosphere of shared learning.

The PITS program enables students not only to discover the art of dramatic language but also how to put these tools of expression into use in their own daily lives.

For more information about *Playwriting in the Schools,* contact:
Playwriting in the Schools
The Public Theater
425 Lafayette Street
New York, NY 10003
(212) 598-7184

WHO AM I
BY MIRIAM VILLANEUVA
AGE 14
JUNIOR HIGH SCHOOL 22

Creature

I am a creature from outer space. I live on Venus. My favorite meal is slime and it tastes delicious. I have long green and purple hair. When I comb it with the cat bones my hair is soft. The only thing that bothers me is my two antennas. I love painting my twenty fingernails and my fifteen toe nails. One feature I like about myself is my six green eyes. I love being me.

DREAM
BY SHAVONTEL CRYSTAL GREEN
AGE 7
P.S. 36

1 Girl
Shavontel

I had a dream that I was hanging with my friends. We went to the store and they stole stuff, so they told me to steal something, too. I said no, because you could go to jail. And anyway I already had money. So they said, "You are not in our gang!" So I said, "So what?" because I didn't want to be in the gang. Some kids rob stuff, but I don't steal. You're supposed to buy things, not steal them! So I told them that I didn't want to be in this bad stealer's gang. I said, "Get away from me! I'm not in this gang! I'm gonna be a normal child!"

MONOLOGUE
BY TERELLA LEE
AGE 11
LYDIA E. HOFFMAN FAMILY RESIDENCE

1 Girl
Terella

I am beautiful. Some people make fun of people because of how they look. But what if someone is talking about you and you know it's not true? If its really bad would you start to cry? That happened to me and I started to cry. My mother looked at me and said, "Why are you crying, if it's not true. Everyone is beautiful. No one is ugly. People say that just to get some attention." I wrote this poem just to say everyone is beautiful in this world.

HOMELESS MONOLOGUE
BY SHARLENE MALDONADO
AGE 13
JUNIOR HIGH SCHOOL 22

1 Girl
Johanna

I'm not ashamed that my father is a homeless man. My friends tell me why do you go to him, when guys are around. But he's my Dad and he always will be. My Dad and Mom broke up because he drinks too much, so he decided to leave. None of his family accepted him, so he decided to live on the stoop of an abandoned building. To this day I love him, and I will never be embarrassed to say to my friends he's my father.

DEAR UNIVERSE, DEAR WORLD
BY TONYA MCKINLEY CROMER
AGE 12
URBAN FAMILY LIVING CENTER

Dear Universe, Dear World,

I need a place to be right now. I feel like no one cares about me. I feel a little bit of love and a little bit of hate. But what I feel can't take me anywhere. I feel bad on the bottom of my feet, and good on the top. I feel nobody cares. This place makes me feel like if I'm in a little dark spot… I'm lost. I can't be seen. Or I can't see anyone's face. I'm in my own world, my special place. So, come to this special place. Come and feel what I feel: Nothing. I can't feel anybody loves me, 'cause there's no one to be with me. I need a little bit of help. Someone there beside me. Push my mind up. I need someone, so come with me in my little special, special place.

I LOVE MY FAMILY/
WHO AM I?
BY GABRIEL HERRERA
AGE 13
JUNIOR HIGH SCHOOL 22

1 Boy
Gabriel

I love my family. My grandfather died. I never knew how much I loved him until he died. I remember a hug my grandfather gave me. I think that was the last hug he ever gave anyone. He loved me, you know. I wish I knew how much I loved him, then. The last hug that he gave me was very long—about a minute. I wish I hadn't pushed him away. Well, I didn't push him away, but I gave a sigh and he let go. I love him.

Who am I? Gabriel Herrera. I am the elephant that roams around in the jungle with its huge body. I am a block of ice that never dies. I am a bald eagle that rules the skies. I am grandfather who never got to live. I am an actor who never got to act. I am a writer who never got to write. I am the fatal beauty that the dying last sees. I am a baby's eyes who first sees his mother. I am the happiness that goes in people. I am me, Gabriel Herrera, the light of my parents' life. I used to be quiet, but now I have a voice.

THE END

A SPECIAL THANKS TO THE CHILDREN WHOSE PHOTOS APPEAR IN CHILDSPLAY

Selene Adorno, Nadezhda Ball, Elektra Carras, Nicolina Dante, Nikki Dowling, Amanda Dunk, Lauren Ellis, Martin Gaston, Alexis Georgiou, Ralph Gigante, Billy Gordon, Kristina Hernandez, Scarlett Johansson, Eva Kiezik, Mark Kleynerman, Julia Livi, Talia Lugacy, Rita Merson, Chanelle Rojas, Victoria Schwartz, Samantha Severin, Lindsey Spielfogel, Alanna Bronx Taubman, Zachary Terzis, and Serena Wilcox.